JAPANESE DEATH POEMS

W9-BTS-600

(Frontispiece).
Calligraphy
"Death"
by Hakuin.
(See p. 6.)

JAPANESE DEATH POEMS

Written by Zen Monks and Haiku Poets
on the Verge of Death

compiled with an Introduction and commentary
by YOEL HOFFMANN

❖

TUTTLE PUBLISHING
Boston • Rutland, Vermont • Tokyo

First published by Tuttle Publishing, an imprint of Periplus Editions (HK) Ltd., with editorial offices at 153 Milk Street, Boston, Massachusetts 02109.

Copyright © 1986 Charles E. Tuttle Publishing Co., Inc.

All rights reserved. No part of this publication may be reproduced or utilized in any form or by any means, electronic or mechanical, including photocopying, recording, or by any information storage and retrieval system, without prior written permission from the publisher.

Library of Congress Catalog Card Number: 85-052347

ISBN: 0-8048-3179-3

Distributed by:

North America, Latin America and Europe
Tuttle Publishing
364 Innovation Drive
North Clarendon, VT 05759-9436
Tel: (802) 773-8930
Fax: (802) 773-6993
Email: info@tuttlepublishing.com
Web site: www.tuttlepublishing.com

Asia Pacific
Berkeley Books Pte. Ltd.
130 Joo Seng Road
#06-01/03 Olivine Building
Singapore 368357
Tel: (65) 6280-3320
Fax: (65) 6280-6290
Email: inquiries@periplus.com.sg
Web site: www.periplus.com

Japan
Tuttle Publishing
Yaekari Building, 3rd Floor
5-4-12 Ōsaki, Shinagawa-ku, Tokyo
Japan 141-0032
Tel: (03) 5437-0171
Fax: (03) 5437-0755
Email: tuttle-sales@gol.com

Indonesia
PT Java Books Indonesia
JI. Kelapa Gading Kirana
Blok A14 No. 17
Jakarta 14240 Indonesia
Tel: (62-21) 451-5351
Fax: (62-21) 453-4987
Email: cs@javabooks.co.id

09 08 07 06 05   17 16 15 14 13
Printed in the United States of America

TUTTLE PUBLISHING ® is a registered trademark of Tuttle Publishing.

❖ *TABLE OF CONTENTS* ❖

Wakaishu ya	O young folk—
shinu ga iya nara	if you fear death,
ima shiniyare	die now!
hito-tabi shineba	Having died once,
mō shinanu zo ya	you won't die again.

(Frontispiece). Calligraphy by Japanese Zen master Hakuin (1685–1768). The poem is written above the character 死 (*shi*, death). (Courtesy of Tanaka Daisaburo and Graphic-sha, Tokyo.)

❖ *ACKNOWLEDGMENTS* ❖

My DEEPEST THANKS *go to Professor Mitsuda Kazunobu of Kyoto University, without whose help and advice I could not have written this book; to Mr. LaVern Lenz, with whose invaluable help this book now appears in English; to my father, Abraham Hoffmann, who read through the manuscript and offered helpful suggestions; and to my good friends, Zen master Hirano Sojo and his wife Hiroko, who opened their home to me and took me in as one of their family.*

I wish to express my gratitude to the Fund for Basic Research administered by the Israel Academy of Sciences and Humanities and to the University of Haifa for their support of the research involved in putting together the book.

For permission to publish in translation the Zen poems anthologized in his Zenso no Yuige *and* Zenso no Shoji, *thanks go to Dr. Furuta Shokin (b. 1911), professor of Hokkaido University and Nihon University, director of Matsugaoka Bunko founded by Daisetsu Suzuki, and author of* Furuta Shokin Chosakushu *(14 vols.) and other works.*

I also wish to thank Mr. Tanaka Daisaburo, the owner of the calligraphy by Hakuin shown in the Frontispiece, and Graphic-sha Publishing Company of Tokyo for the use of their photograph of that work.

Finally, I would like to acknowledge the assistance rendered by members of the editorial staff of the Charles E. Tuttle Company, who were able to refine many points of detail throughout the manuscript.

❖ PREFACE ❖

Death in itself is nothing; but we fear
To be we know not what, we know not where.
—DRYDEN

Death may indeed be nothing in itself, yet the conscious-
ness of death is in most cultures very much a part of life.
This is perhaps nowhere more true than in Japan, where
the approach of death has given rise to a centuries-old
tradition of writing a "death poem." Hundreds of such
poems, many with a commentary describing the poet
and the circumstances of his or her death, have been
gathered from Japanese sources and translated here into
English, the great majority of them for the first time.
As poems, they share the beauty of a poetry that has
already gained the admiration of the West; as death
poems, they reflect important aspects of a culture that is
still largely unfamiliar to many Western readers.

Part One of this book explores the tradition of writing
a death poem against a detailed background of attitudes
toward death throughout the cultural history of Japan.

Part Two contains death poems by Zen Buddhist monks, and Part Three is an anthology of haiku, hitherto unassembled even in Japan, written by some three hundred twenty Japanese poets on the verge of death. The death poems of most of the better-known haiku poets, and many by lesser-known poets as well, are included in this last part.

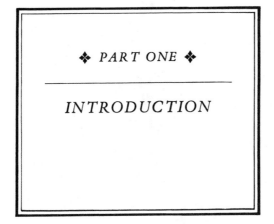

❖ *PART ONE* ❖

INTRODUCTION

Note: Throughout the book, Japanese names are rendered in traditional order, that is, surname followed by given name. Japanese words are romanized in the Hepburn system; macrons, for long vowels, are retained only in the transcriptions of the poems, to show correct syllable count.

❖ *INTRODUCTION* ❖

THE POETRY OF JAPAN

The earliest known examples of Japanese lyric poetry are verses found in the first records of Japanese history, the *Kojiki* (Record of ancient matters), completed in 712 A.D. Simple in structure and free of formal constraints, these verses celebrate the beauty of nature, love and longing, and loyalty to the sovereign in what seem like bursts of spontaneous expression. Japan's first anthology of poetry, the *Man'yoshu* (Collection of myriad words), appeared at the end of the eighth century. Containing more than four thousand poems, it seems to have been compiled by court officials, and yet, along with verses composed by emperors and noblemen, there is the work of monks, of warriors, and even of common people. It seems that the writing of poetry was not the pastime of an exclusive few with special talent, nor was it confined to any particular class. The lyricism of the *Man'yoshu* is simple and direct, and its themes—the beauty of nature, love and parting, wine and merrymaking, grief and sorrow over the transience of all things—have remained unchanged throughout Japan's history. The vigorous style of this early poetry, however, soon gave way to "court poetry," in which artifice, wit, and subtle plays on words often overshadow strong emotions.

The poems in the *Man'yoshu* are of two primary forms: the *tanka,* "short poem," a verse of thirty-one syllables in five lines, the syllables distributed in the pattern 5–7–5–7–7; and the *choka,* "long poem," also consisting of five- and seven-syllable lines, but indefinite in length. In the years following the appearance of the *Man'yoshu,* the long form was retained only for elegies, and the tanka became the conventional form of poetry.

Throughout the Heian period (794–1185), the writing of poetry became more and more popular among the nobility. Poetic competitions were held in the emperor's court, and several anthologies of poetry were compiled. The best known of these is the *Kokinshu* (or *Kokinwakashu,* Collection of ancient and new Japanese poems), put together under the auspices of Emperor Daigo in 905. Already under the influence of Chinese culture, the poems here are more sophisticated, more trenchant, and wittier than those of the *Man'yoshu.* Most of them were composed by court noblemen, some by the emperor himself, and by Buddhist priests and monks. Poetry at the time of the *Kokinshu* had become a major occupation of noblemen and ladies of the court, poetic ability often being a means of advancement to positions of power and prestige. Inclusion of one's verses in the imperial anthology was a great distinction. In addition to anthologies published by decree of the emperor, collections of poems by single individuals appeared as well. Rival schools of poetry arose, each adhering to different aesthetic ideals, each with its own masters who guarded the "secrets of the poetic art" and passed them on to only a chosen few. Writing poetry had gradually come to require more knowledge than before, and it thus became the pastime only of those with the leisure to pursue it, the nobles.

Chinese influence on Japanese poetry began to be felt in the eighth century. Chinese culture reached a peak during the T'ang dynasty (618–907), and the Japanese eagerly adopted Chinese patterns of thought in government, philosophy, literature, and art. Members of the court and other educated people felt compelled to express themselves in the Chinese language, which enjoyed a status much like that of Latin in medieval Europe. But Chinese poetry, though much admired and studied with persistence and devotion, never effected a significant change in native forms of poetry. The Japanese merely took on, beside their traditional tanka form, a foreign genre—the *kanshi,* "Chinese poem." Writing poems in classical Chinese has persisted among the learned up to the present century, but it can hardly be said that the Japanese have made a significant contribution to Chinese poetry. This is understandable given the considerable difference between the Chinese and Japanese languages. Although the Japanese adopted the Chinese system of writing, and although thousands of Chinese words passed into their written and spoken language, very few Japanese poets really mastered Chinese.

Until the sixteenth century, nearly all poetry written in Japanese took the thirty-one-syllable tanka form. The development from tanka to the more well-known haiku can be understood in connection with the *renga,* "linked poem," which provides a kind of historical tie between the tanka and haiku structures. Toward the end of the Heian period, there had been a tendency among tanka poets to divide their poems into two units with syllabic counts of 5–7–5 (three lines) and

7–7 (two lines), each unit containing a poetic image of its own. During the fourteenth century, the *renga* developed alongside the tanka. Two or more poets would take part in writing *renga,* composing, in turns, verses of seventeen (5–7–5) and fourteen (7–7) syllables. Each such verse is linked to the preceding and following verses in accordance with strict conventions by means of images, associations, or plays on words. The results of these gatherings are "chain poems" sometimes scores of verses long—collective creations that changed the writing of poetry from an art with social functions to a genuinely social pastime.

Before long, two styles of poetry arose in the *renga* tradition, each differing in the class and temperament of its participants. One style tended toward rigid, formal rules, serious subject matter, and refined language, in the traditional manner of court poetry. The other, which prevailed increasingly during the sixteenth century, was formally less rigorous and more popular in tone. Poets writing *haikai no renga,* the latter style, made use of images drawn from everyday life, expressed simply and often humorously. This was the style adopted by Matsuo Basho (1644–94), one of the greatest of haiku poets. He and his pupils often chose to compose only the opening passage of a *renga,* the *hokku,* "opening phrase," as a verse in itself, forgoing the rest of the chain. In this manner the opening unit of seventeen syllables in three lines came to be considered a poem in its own right, and more and more poets began to test their talents with it rather than with the tanka. This shortened style was at times called *haikai* and later received the name it holds today—*haiku.*

If we except *renga,* a special form of "collective poetry," and the Chinese poem, which is ultimately a grafted branch of Japanese culture, we find two major forms of poetry in Japan at the beginning of the sixteenth century: the thirty-one-syllable tanka and the seventeen-syllable haiku.* These two compact structures have accounted for almost all of Japanese poetry. Even among the Japanese, however, there are those who feel that these structures are too brief to express the full range of human emotions. In the nineteenth century, when Japan opened her doors to the influence of Western culture, some Japanese poets began to experiment with foreign styles, setting no specific limits as to form and length. Traditional Japanese poetry was never abandoned, however, and though imitations of Western modes were made with varying degrees of success, none of them capture the beauty of the native forms. Today "modern poetry" in the manner of the West is written by only a few hundred Japanese, most of them from among the intelligentsia, but millions of people from all ranks of society write tanka and haiku.

It should perhaps be mentioned that there is no direct historical link between the early Zen monks whose Chinese poems are presented in Part Two of this book and the haiku poets of the sixteenth century onward, represented in Part Three. The attitude expressed by haiku poets, however, often reflects Zen Buddhist elements; indeed, many haiku poets

* Two styles complementary to the tanka and haiku later grew up beside these forms. The *kyoka,* "mad poem," is a satirical tanka not usually based on an image from nature at all; this form was especially popular in the latter half of the eighteenth century. The *senryu,* named after the genre's creator, Karai Senryu (1718–90), is a haiku that satirizes human foibles. The *senryu* is usually written in haiku form, but may be even shorter, in two lines of seven syllables each.

took a deep interest in Zen Buddhism, some to the point of donning a robe and wandering up and down Japan begging rice from door to door, after the manner of Zen monks. Despite the historical gap and the consequent cultural differences, a strong spiritual kinship can be discerned between the farewell poems written in Chinese by Zen monks and many of the poems written by haiku poets. By contrast, tanka, at least with regard to death poems written in this genre, tend to reflect a rather different perception of the world. These poems are treated only in this Introduction.

In order to understand further the background of the death poetry of Zen monks and haiku poets, we shall first examine the structure of Chinese poetry, then distinguish further between the tanka and the haiku forms, and finally, discuss the peculiar characteristics of haiku.

CHINESE POETRY

There are several general principles governing classical Chinese poetry. The number of "words," that is, characters, in a line is fixed; poems of five characters per line and of seven characters per line are the most common. Most poems are rhymed and have definite patterns of tone, Chinese being a tone language. (When Chinese words entered Japanese, the tones were ignored, but Japanese writers of Chinese poetry developed systems of symbols to keep track of the tones for the purpose of writing the poems correctly.) Syntactically, the lines do not depend on one another; each line is a separate phrase. There are short poems of fixed length and longer ones that are divided more or less into verses.

Let us take as an example a poem entitled "Self-Consolation" by the poet Li Po (701–62). The poem is four lines long, each line composed of five characters. This is the poem in literal translation:

facing	wine	not	distinguish	twilight
fall	flower(s)	pile up	I/my	robe
drunk	rise	walk	valley	moon
bird(s)	return	man	also	rare

In a free translation, we may read:

Lost in wine, I did not notice dusk descending
Petals dropped and piled up on my robe
Drunk, I rise and walk the moonlit valley
The birds have gone, and people too are few.

TANKA AND HAIKU

Because most Japanese words end in one of five vowels, rhymed poetry would be very bland. Japanese poems are not in fact rhymed, but another device, the alternation of five- and seven-syllable lines, creates a rhythm peculiar to Japanese poetry.

Most tanka contain two poetic images. The first is taken from nature; the second, which may precede, follow, or be woven into the first, is a kind of meditative complement to the nature image. Tanka produce a certain dreamlike effect, presenting images of reality without that definite quality of "realness" often possessed by photographs or drawings, as if the image proceeded directly from the mind of the dreamer. The tanka poet may be likened to a person holding two mirrors in his hands, one reflecting a scene from nature, the other reflecting himself as he holds the first mirror. The tanka thus provides a look at nature, but it regards the observer of nature as well. The haiku is not merely a compact tanka: the four-teen syllables dropped from the tanka, so to speak, in order to produce a haiku, are in effect the mirror that reflects the poet. Haiku shattered the self-reflecting mirror, leaving in the hands of the poet only the mirror that reflects nature.

To demonstrate the difference between the forms, let us look at a tanka written by Ki-no-Tsurayuki (870–945), a court noble, poet, and one of the scholars who compiled the *Kokinshu*:

Winds passing	*Hana no ka ni*
through the shaded grove	*koromo wa fukaku*
weigh down	*narinikeri*
my robe with	*ko-no-shita kage no*
the scent of blossoms.	*kaze no ma ni ma ni*

At first sight, the poem seems to present no more than a poetic image drawn from nature, but in fact it dwells upon that image more than would be the case in haiku. As it stands the poem refers to the location of the speaker, "the shaded grove," and to the manner in which the scent of blossoms seeps into his gown (lit., whenever the wind blows). The in-terweaving of these elements creates a rather complex state-ment which cannot be grasped without some meditative effort. Were a haiku poet of seven hundred years later asked to distill this tanka into a haiku, he would probably choose the surprising image of flower scent adding to the weight of his robe, and restrict the poem to this seasonal image of spring:

> My robe
> grows heavy
> with the scent of blossoms.

We can apply the same principle to the following tanka by Fujiwara-no-Yoshitsune (1169–1206). He prefaced his poem with the title "An Animal, Emblem of Love."

> These days   *Konogoro no*
> my inmost thoughts recall   *kokoro no soko o*
> an autumn sunset   *yoso ni miba*
> when the deer's call   *shika naku nobe no*
> echoes over fields.   *aki no yūgure*

A haiku poet might have suppressed the contemplative beginning and contented himself with the second part (the last two lines of the original):

> Autumn sunset:
> a deer's call
> echoes over fields.

We conclude this demonstration with a poem by an emperor's wife, Eifuku Mon'in (1271–1342), who became a nun at the age of forty-five and dedicated her time to poetry:

> Thus night fell.   *Kakushite zo*
> Yesterday as well   *kinō mo kureshi*
> the sun went down   *yama-no-ha no*
> behind the mountain peaks   *irihi no ato ni*
> and bells rang.   *kane no koegoe*

If we drop the philosophical opening (the first two lines of the original), we obtain the same poetic image in haiku form:

> The sun goes down
> behind the mountain peaks
> and bells ring.

THE HAIKU

The haiku is probably the shortest verse form found in either the East or the West. Most words in Japanese consist of more than one syllable, so the number of words in a haiku is remarkably small—from five to eight or nine altogether. Haiku are not rhymed; the only formal rule (which is sometimes violated) is the fixed number of syllables. Words are not usually divided between the end of one line and the beginning of the next, so each of the lines may contain from one to three words. Though a good haiku may contain more than one sentence, it always evokes only one poetic image. This image is essentially descriptive, and great clarity of vision is required of the poet in order to create it, so to speak, with only a few strokes of the brush. Since about the sixteenth century, three conventions have become universally accepted: (1) the haiku describes a single state or event; (2) the time of the haiku is the present; and (3) the haiku refers to images connected to one of the four seasons.

Let us take as an example a haiku written by Mizuta Masahide (1657–1723) after his storehouse had burned down:

> *Ku ra*   *ya ke te*
> 1 2   3 4 5
> storehouse burn

> *sa wa ru   mo no   na ki*
> 1 2 3   4 5   6 7
> obstruct   thing   no
>
> *tsu ki mi   ka na*
> 1 2 3   4 5
> moon-view   (exclamation)

In the translation here, I have preserved the 5–7–5 syllable form (compare an alternate translation on p. 240):

> My storehouse burned down—
> now nothing stands between me
> and the moon above.

Haiku are sometimes meticulously translated into English with exactly seventeen syllables, often at the expense of accuracy. But even when such a translation remains as true to the original as a free rendering, the poetic achievement is slight, for the reader who has not been raised in a haiku-saturated culture is unlikely to appreciate the poem's peculiar 5–7–5 beat rhythm as keenly as one who has. Other translators forgo the convention of counting syllables and replace it with another convention, rhyme. A successfully rhymed haiku may indeed contribute to the beauty of the translation, but because of the extreme brevity of haiku style, rhyming more often than not makes a jingle of the poem. The translations in this book are nearly all in free verse. The one structural precept adhered to throughout is that each haiku is translated in three lines—usually a short, a long, and a short one again. While free style lessens the number of formal constraints on the translator, it demands greater attention to the choice and arrangement of words.

Formal considerations aside, how can we account for the peculiar quality of the haiku poem? Basho, foremost among haiku poets, said, "About the pine, learn from the pine; about the reed, learn from the reed." He suggests perhaps that the poet must become unconscious of himself so as to see the object of his poem with absolute clarity, as it is in and of itself. A similar approach is suggested by a modern scholar, Kenneth Yasuda:

> When one happens to see a beautiful sunset or lovely flower, for instance, one is often so delighted that one merely stands still. This state of mind might be called "ah-ness," for the beholder can only give one breath-long exclamation of delight: "Ah!" The object has seized him and he is aware only of the shapes, the colors, the shadows. . . . There is here no time or place explicitly for reflection for judgments, or for the observer's feelings. . . . To render such a moment is the intent of all haiku, and the discipline of the form.[1]

In haiku, then, there is an attempt to "say something without saying it." That which remains unsaid tells more than the words and yet is unclear without them. Words are used like the few lines of ink in Japanese and Chinese landscapes that emphasize the vastness of the scene. Whatever the seasonal image of a haiku, there is something in it of a wintry landscape: we cannot discern its features if an occasional point does not stand out against the snow, a point of color that puts the white view in relief. It is at this point that the haiku stands, though its significance, like that of the point in the drawing, lies in the grandeur of the surrounding scene.

Much has been said and written about the "haiku moment"
—that it blurs the distinction between "subject" and "object,"
"self" and "other"; that in it the perception of the essential
and the accidental, of the beautiful and the ugly, disappears;
that it reflects things as they are in themselves. It has further
been asserted that in haiku, place and time are always here
and now, and yet all places and all times, no place and no time.
There is without doubt something of the truth in such ob-
servations, but the point of stating them is questionable, and
the harm certain. Haiku poetry resounds with endless mean-
ings just because it so often attains that perfect simplicity
sought for in philosophy, religion, literature, and art.

> Darkening sea: *Umi kurete*
> a mallard's call   *kamo no koe*
> sounds dimly white.   *honoka ni shiroshi*

It is mid-winter, at twilight, and Basho stands on the seashore.
Patches of light on the waves still reflect the setting sun, and
wild ducks call: for Basho, sound and light merge.

The following poem, also by Basho, brings out the mys-
tery in another seasonal image, this one related to spring.
The contour is blurred, and even the little that appears is
wrapped in haze:

> Spring has come—   *Haru nare ya*
> a nameless mountain   *na mo naki yama no*
> wrapped in mist.   *usugasumi*

The following poem by Yosa Buson (1716–83), a painter
as well as a poet, is more colorful. His is a spring image, too:

The springtime sun	*Yamadori no*
sets, treading	*o o fumu haru no*
on a mountain pheasant's tail.	*irihi kana*

Kobayashi Issa (1763–1827), of whose poetry the Japanese are very fond, paints an autumn scene in which the fixed and the changing alternate:

Autumn wind:	*Akikaze ya*
the mountain's shadow	*hyorohyoro yama no*
quivering.	*kagebōshi*

The next haiku, by Oshima Ryota (1718–87), contains an autumnal image ("moon," unless otherwise qualified, signifies the moon of autumn). For a fraction of a second, the gap between reality and illusion, the eternal and the momentary, closes:

Moon in the water	*Mizu no tsuki*
somersaults	*mondori utte*
and streams away.	*nagarekeri*

The haiku poet observes what others scarcely see. How many of us would have noticed what Shiba Fukio (1903–30) describes in the next poem—the split-second gap between the horse's first step and the movement of the carriage?

A barley wagon	*Mugi-guruma*
lags—then leaps	*uma ni okurete*
behind the horse.	*ugoki izu*

Finally, there are those who maintain that a poem as short as the haiku cannot convey the depth and complexity of our feelings. But hasn't Ochi Etsujin (b. 1656) captured, in the following poem, an entire "scene from a marriage"?

Autumn evening:	*Aki no kure*
"Isn't it time," she comes and asks,	*hi ya tomosan to*
"to light the lantern?"	*toi ni kuru*

DEATH AND ITS POETRY
IN THE CULTURAL HISTORY OF JAPAN

In Japan, as elsewhere in the world, it has become customary to write a will in preparation for one's death. But Japanese culture is probably the only one in the world in which, in addition to leaving a will, a tradition of writing a "farewell poem to life" *(jisei)* took root and became widespread. If we examine the wills left by the Japanese throughout their history, we occasionally find instructions and appeals to survivors concerning their moral or social conduct; usually, however, wills deal only with the division of property. It has been suggested, then, that the death poem is perhaps a kind of salutation. The Japanese learn hundreds of polite forms of address so as to be prepared for every possible social situation, and status and prestige are measured, to a great extent, by one's ability to find the greeting most appropriate to the circumstances. Should we then regard death poems as a final salute to those who remain alive, the last act of politeness? In fact, death poems reveal that before death, the Japanese tend rather to break the restraints of politeness that hold them back during their lifetime; we must comb through hundreds of death poems in order to find one or two written in the style customary for polite greetings. Neither material nor social concerns come to the fore. Death poems seem to reflect, more than anything else, the *spiritual* legacy of the Japanese.

DEATH: BELIEFS AND PRACTICES

We might well ask ourselves, first, how the Japanese think about death and dying. When one studies the history of Japan, one cannot help but notice the great extent to which the events and changes of each historical period contribute something of lasting value to the variegated whole which we call culture. Moreover, different traditions which take root first in only one class or rank of society eventually influence all other social levels as well.

As an illustration of this point I cannot resist mentioning the elderly landlady of the house in Kyoto where I stayed for several years. She had laid the foundations of her house in a ceremony conducted by a Shinto priest. The ritual fixed the orientation of the house in accordance with the dictates of Shinto gods, and a heap of stones erected in her yard is a symbol of their presence. Though the woman herself had been married in a Shinto ceremony, her daughter was married in a Christian church, and her close relatives were buried in the cemetery of a Buddhist temple. On the wall of her room a Buddhist family altar *(butsudan)* is fixed, bearing the names of her dead ancestors. She brings rice and other offerings to them in small dishes, a custom with roots in Shinto. Once a month a Buddhist priest comes to her house to offer prayers to her ancestors in the belief that if their spirits remain at peace, they will influence her life to the good (also from Shinto). As one who respects her forebears both living and dead, and who thus fulfills the first precept of a moral life (a Confucian concept), she hopes to be reborn after death in the Pure Land in the West, the Buddhist paradise. Every Sunday she goes to a nearby Christian church and offers a prayer to Jesus. And thus one elderly woman pays deep respect to each and every one of the many guests and residents that have made their way throughout history into the "open house" of Japanese culture—Shinto deities, various avatars of Buddha, Confucian ancestors, and the God of Christianity. It is precisely this generous spirit of the Japanese, who without qualms embrace one idea and its opposite at once, that reveals a deeper understanding, an understanding that life and death cannot be formulated in a single idea, because reality is more complex than any logic, and at the same time so much more simple.

In the Japanese language, use of the stark term "death" *(shi)* in reference to individuals is rare. The Japanese refer, rather, to the particular kind of death: *shinju,* lover's suicide; *junshi,* a warrior's martyrdom for his lord; *senshi,* death in war; *roshi,* death from old age; etc. These expressions link the death to the kind of life led by the person and to the circumstances of his death. It is common to refer to the deceased as a Buddha *(hotoke),* a reminder of the belief that death purifies a person from the ignorance and lust that sully mankind.

Many Japanese prepare for death as soon as they feel their time is near. A will is written to settle the distribution of property and keepsakes among relatives and friends. For the most part, these arrangements take place in an atmosphere of serenity, with almost pleasurable expectation of the voyage to the next world. These preparations do not merely reflect a realistic attitude toward circumstances; they also inspire calmness in the dying, allowing them to settle spiritual accounts and to ask pardon for past misdeeds. Orthodox Buddhists about to die sometimes copy sacred scriptures, usually the *Hannya-Shin-gyo,* a collection of late Buddhist writings expounding the doctrine that the essence of all things is emptiness, or void. Many people, and principally those who have cared for poetry, then write their death poems, sometimes in their very last moments.

Much importance is attached to funeral ceremonies. The dead person whose funeral has not been properly performed is liable, the Japanese believe, to have difficulty crossing over to the world beyond and may therefore plague the living. If a person has been killed, the murderer must be seized and punished, lest the victim's vengeance-seeking spirit haunt the scene of its death or the house of its relatives. Today, burial in the ground is practiced mainly in rural areas where land is relatively abundant; in most regions of the country, however, cremation is the rule. Whether the corpse is burned or buried, the location of the grave is of great importance: land on which one's family has lived for generations is preferred.

According to Japanese tradition, the deceased does not pass over immediately to a world from which no return is possible. One belief is that the spirit of the dead person remains near the world of the living for forty-nine days; another is that the spirit hovers on the borders of the world of the living for some decades and only then, if all goes well, does it merge into the greater order of the cosmos. This accounts for the popular belief that contact can be made between the living and the dead. Up to recent times, the Japanese have believed in the power of female mediums *(miko)* who call the dead on behalf of the living. Most Japanese address their dead, either at the gravesite or at the family altar in the home, and simply talk to them. They tell them of marriages, births, and deaths in the family, include them in joyful occasions, complain to them about other members of the family and even—who knows?— heed their advice.

The Bon Festival, which is celebrated in midsummer, is essentially a Buddhist holiday. However, it includes some elements of Shinto, and is imbued with the Confucian spirit of reverence for one's ancestors. During the holiday, people return to their place of birth, visit family graves, and pray for the peace of the souls of their ancestors. At the time of the Bon Festival, as during the celebration of New Year's Day and the equinoxes, it is said that the spirits of the dead return to their ancestral homes to see how their relatives are faring. In preparation for this, an effigy of a horse is made from eggplants, cucumbers, and reeds and is put on the family altar. The dead arrive on the back of the horse, and when the holiday is over, they return to their world in small wood and paper boats bearing a lighted candle, which are set to sail on bodies of water.

Students of Japanese culture cannot fail to discover that for the Japanese the group often takes precedence over the individual. The group is usually the family, those tied by blood relationships, but the concept of the group widened in the course of time to include the clan, and later, the entire nation as represented by the emperor or the shogun. As the group is most important in life, it is the group that grants the Japanese his existence in the afterlife as well. The notion of an individual salvation has relatively little place in the Japanese view of death. (Religions in Japan do not present the picture, so familiar in Judaism, Christianity, and Islam, of the deity as a force superior to nature, observing the individual and judging him after death for his most private thoughts.) In Western societies, the idea that dying is a purely personal matter may be the cause of the near taboo on the very subject of death, much like the taboo on the subject of sex. The Japanese belief that even death is a group-related event reduces, perhaps, the fear of dying, for the dead remain, as it were, within the boundaries of this world and continue to share in the daily lives of their relatives.

So far only a few of the many Japanese customs and beliefs concerning death have been mentioned. What are some of the historical and cultural sources of these views? We can still find in Japan today the remains of huge mausoleums built for rulers and nobles in the first centuries A.D. No written records exist from this early period, but archeological findings indicate that the ancient inhabitants of the Japanese islands viewed death as various forms of voyage, whether underground, into the mountains, beyond the horizon of the sea, or into the sky. The magnificent tombs were built, apparently, to house the deceased upon their return from the "voyage of death."

The earliest written source of knowledge about the Japanese perception of death is the *Kojiki*. Life is portrayed in this work as teeming activity, a scene of violent clashes among intensely strong forces of fertility and creation. It is the story of godlike men and women who receive their vitality from nature spirits. Death is the gray side of the picture—a dark, polluted, and fearful plane. We find in the *Kojiki* an account of a visit to the realm of the dead—a story which mirrors in many ways that of Orpheus. Izanagi and Izanami are brother and sister who marry one another by command of the gods. Themselves deities, they create, so says the ancient myth, the islands of Japan. Izanami gives birth from various parts of her body to many gods, including those of rivers and seas and those of trees and hills. After delivering the god of fire, she dies. The grief-stricken Izanagi journeys to Yomi, the land of the dead, where he finds her and entreats her to come back with him. She replies that she cannot, for she has "eaten of the furnace" of Yomi. Nevertheless, she promises to speak with the gods of Yomi about her wish to return with Izanagi, imploring him not to look upon her in the meanwhile. He breaks this taboo and sees her body, in which "maggots were squirming."[2] Izanagi returns alone to the land of the living and performs a rite of purification.

This myth acquaints us with beliefs about death in the centuries preceding the compilation of the *Kojiki*. Scholars disagree as to whether Yomi represents merely the burial place of the dead in underground rock-chambers, or a separate subterranean land. The dead seem to wander freely from place to place as do the living, but one is forbidden to look at them. Corpses arouse feelings of pollution, of uncleanliness. This attitude of death as "unclean" reflected in the *Kojiki* remains alive even today in, for example, the practice of sprinkling salt over oneself after one returns home from a funeral. Shinto priests rarely conduct funeral services, and when, occasionally, a Shinto burial does take place, the officiating priest is considered unclean for three days thereafter.

Reflecting an altogether different approach to death, another hero of the *Kojiki*, a semi-legendary figure named Yamato Takeru-no-Mikoto (second cent. A.D.?) turns into a great white bird when he dies. His wife and children chase after the bird over sea and shore, cutting their feet on bamboo stumps and singing songs of mourning all the while. Other heroes dive into lakes like water birds and disappear.

It would seem that at this stage of their culture, the Japanese had not yet formulated clear-cut ideas about death and the life beyond it. In both the *Kojiki* and the *Man'yoshu* different depictions of the afterlife occur side by side: as a descent into Yomi, as an ascent into the skies, as a voyage by sail on the ocean, or as a journey into the mountains. In the latter work, the dead are also represented by clouds and mist, reflecting, perhaps, the newly introduced custom of cremation. The conception of the land of the dead as a subterranean realm most certainly arises from the practice of burying corpses in the ground. The inhabitants of one area of Japan, present-day Shimane Prefecture, even believed that a certain large boulder found there covered the entrance into Yomi. Remains of human skeletons and other bones used in rites of augury have been found together near this rock, suggesting that it was the site of ceremonies to conciliate spirits of the dead. Elsewhere, in prehistoric graves of southern Asia, boats were drawn either in the shape of birds or with birdlike prows; sometimes the oarsmen themselves were pictured in bird costumes. Bird bones have been found resting on the chests of ancient human skeletons, and the *Kojiki* alludes to a custom whereby mourners dress up as birds. The evidence suggests, then, that the ancient Japanese believed that the dead turned into birds, or perhaps that birds carried them to another world. To this day it is thought that ravens embody the souls of the dead, and that the cuckoo is a harbinger of death. Many death poems reflect these beliefs.

Where did the ancient Japanese, a largely maritime people, send their dead? The "birds of death" sailed sometimes from the eastern shore, sometimes from the western one, out toward the horizon where sea and sky meet. Did the prehistoric Japanese, who were sun-worshipers, believe that the huge fiery ball which rose from the sea every morning or sank beneath it at night (depending on the position of the region, either on the Pacific Ocean or on the Sea of Japan) was the destination of their dead? Traces of a belief that the land of the dead lies over the sea can still be found in the ceremonies of the Bon Festival, during which, as previously mentioned, the dead who have come to visit their relatives return in small paper boats that the living set sail upon bodies of water.

Of all the beliefs concerning death in ancient Japan, however, the most persistent is that which connects it to mountains. From the very beginning mountains were considered the dwelling-places of gods, and were held sacred as such. The summits of mountains were sites for Shinto shrines and, later, for Buddhist temples. Might the ancient Japanese have seen in mountain peaks the points of contact between the gods, who originate in the sun, and men, who dwell on the ground? The Japanese word for Shinto gods is *kami,* which signifies "the top" as well—a hint, perhaps, that the gods look out from mountain peaks below to the narrow plains inhabited by people.

Not death, however, but life is the province of Shinto gods. In parts of northern Japan, mountain deities are worshiped also as gods of birth, and in Aomori Prefecture, also in the north, maturation ceremonies for youths are held in the mountains. There is evidence in classical literature that mountain sites were chosen for betrothal ceremonies as well. It is believed in many areas in Japan that in spring, mountain gods become gods of the field and descend to the plains to protect crops, returning to their mountain homes only in autumn after the harvest. Mountains are thus both the source of life and the place to which life returns. No wonder then that the Japanese, wishing to draw near to this source even in death, preferred to bury their dead some distance from their villages, high up in the mountains. There, where the gods dwell, the dead dwell also, overseeing the habitations of the living. This accounts for the belief, still strong among the Japanese today, that at least the first part of the death journey leads through mountains. Until recently, the dead were even dressed in straw sandals in anticipation of the walk over "Death Mountain" *(shide no yama)*. And like other such beliefs, the one representing death as a mountain journey is reflected in many death poems.

The outlook of the ancient Japanese, then, was basically optimistic. The Buddhist message that the world is a fleeting illusion had not yet reached their ears: this life is a substantial reality, drawing its vitality from gods who reside in nature. The unbridgeable abyss between life and death had not yet opened up, and the dying apparently believed that they would return, by one means or another, to the land of the living.

At the end of the seventh century, Buddhism spread to Japanese soil. The Japanese began to cremate their dead, the smoke rising from their bodies symbolizing the birth of a new perspective on death. This world was no longer the best of all possible worlds, but a polluted one from which the dead soar to another place, the Pure Land *(jodo)* in the West, ruled by Amida, the Buddha of Everlasting Light. Early Buddhist writings contain blood-chilling descriptions of the many and cruel torments awaiting the wicked after death—but the Japanese, in the innocent and optimistic manner so characteristic of them, soon found the means of salvation: it would be sufficient to call Buddha's name before dying in order to be saved from hell. Moreover, dying itself was seen as a process of purification and atonement; at death, everyone became a Buddha.

In the early part of the ninth century, Buddhist philosophy strengthened its hold on Japanese culture. Some Japanese, braving great hardships, sailed to China and studied for years at the feet of Chinese sages for the sole purpose of understanding sacred teachings. Chinese religious teachers and scholars were received like royalty in Japan, and monks founded sects in monasteries built atop high mountain peaks. Buddhism soon found its way into the nobility. Emperors abdicated their thrones to retire within monastery walls; noblewomen shaved their heads and became Buddhist nuns. Writers of the Nara (710–94) and Heian (794–1185) periods never wearied of likening man's life to that of a flower which scarcely blossoms before withering, to dewdrops that evaporate at sunrise, or to a fading illusion or dream. Fleetingness characterized not only the outward forms of nature, but also inward nature; nothing is fixed, nothing is stable. The great literary works of the Heian period, most notably the *Genji Monogatari* (The tale of Genji) by Murasaki Shikibu (*c*. 978–*c*. 1014) and the diaries of court ladies, all describe the world of men and nature alike as a dream or a phantasm.

The Japanese love for nature, however, precluded any escape into abstraction; that which is formless and colorless has no solace for the heart. The idea of transience, expressed in the Buddhist literature of India by the sight of putrefying corpses and rotten food, is conveyed by the Japanese through images of the changing seasons. Though there be no metaphysical salvation in the spectacles of nature, these afford at least a kind of aesthetic salvation. Sights of winter and autumn fill one with melancholy; sights of spring with sorrow for the dying blossoms. And though we may find mention here and there of the eternal peace that lies beyond the world of the senses, the Japanese does not believe, in the depths of his heart, in a world with no spring and no autumn. Grief for the ephemeral gives way to resignation and even to full acceptance of the transient nature of things. It is therefore understandable that the Japanese should pursue, during the Heian period, the Tendai branch of Buddhism, which holds the entire world to be Buddha, with Buddha's nature dwelling everywhere—in mountains, rivers, grass, and trees. Scholars avidly studied Chinese Taoist philosophy, which sees the source of man's being in nature with its changing seasons. Furthermore, the Japanese managed to temper Buddhism's fundamental pessimism with elements from Shinto. In the Buddhist literature of Japan even the Pure Land in the West is often described as a land of beautiful natural scenery.

Some Western scholars, perhaps with a trace of Christian condescension, have called Japanese mysticism "natural," distinguishing it from "spiritual" mysticism. And yet how wise and humane is the culture that does not contrive an otherworldly supreme being to rule this world, the only one we know. One might ask what there is to be gained from a "spiritual" sovereign who disturbs the peace of man with commands to act one way or another, promising in exchange an eternal world where scent, shape, and color never enter. Indeed, even today the Japanese share a deep identification with nature. This is not nature as understood by Western religions, the work of a creator who stands apart from his work, but nature bursting with vitality, appearing and disappearing in cycles of life and death, of summer and winter, spring and fall. The Japanese aspire to clarity of awareness, as of a mirror reflecting natural phenomena in its many forms. And anyone who has seen a Japanese stand silently for a good hour to view the blossoming cherries in spring and the reddening maples in fall, or to gaze at the full moon in the autumn sky, knows that this is no mere gesture of aesthetic appreciation, but an act of worship.

During the Kamakura period (1185–1392), the government of Japan passed from the nobles to the class of the warriors, or samurai, and the world view of the latter gradually came to dominate Japanese culture. Alongside the lyrical images of flower, dew, and dream so favored by the nobility, there appeared a somewhat contradictory idea of life as the scene of heroic deeds and unswerving loyalty to one's lord. The mosaic of samurai-class attitudes prevalent from the twelfth to the nineteenth centuries abounds with seemingly incongruous notions: that the world is like a dream; that the Pure Land in the West awaits believers; that the highest virtue is faithfulness to the clan and its ruler.

The sources of some of these beliefs can be found, in part, in the several schools of Buddhist thought which flourished during the Kamakura period. Among the samurai class, the Jodo, or Pure Land, sects of Buddhism were the most followed, but the elite of the samurai developed a taste for Zen Buddhism as well. This was due not only to the exotic attractions of Zen, but also to its more "masculine" approach to life. Zen recognizes, in contrast to other Buddhist sects, no higher external power. The solution to life's enigma is to be found not outside oneself, but within, in one's mind. One must purify one's consciousness and see reality as it is, in its "suchness." And pure reality, as seen through an enlightened mind, does not admit of such polarites as "life" and "death."

The well-known method of suicide of the samurai, *seppuku,* or *harakiri* (lit., splitting the stomach), often followed from a commitment to certain elements of Zen philosophy. Judaism, Christianity, and Islam all forbid their followers to kill themselves, suicide being looked upon as rebellion against divine will. Instead of divine will, Buddhism conceived of karma—fate as determined by a man's own character and past actions. If one's karma has brought one to the verge of death, what is more natural than to seal one's present existence—which is no more than a single scene in a many-act play of metamorphoses—with a courageous deed that will insure better karma in the next incarnation? In the eyes of a Zen Buddhist, suicide of this sort may even indicate enlightenment, since one who sets no store by either life or death is likely to be liberated from the karmic cycle of births and deaths.

That many samurai leaders in the Kamakura period leaned toward Zen is reflected clearly in their death poems, some of which are translated below. However, sacrificing one's life for one's lord or for the clan is also a Confucian ideal. The individual who dies "appropriately," according to all the rites and ceremonies, sanctifies the name of the entire group. Thus, even a person who has been a "black sheep" during life is taken back, at death, into the bosom of the "family." The tendency to surround self-imposed death with a halo of beauty is seen not only with the suicide of samurai, but that of lovers as well. Death by suicide was condoned for those caught in dilemmas from which they could not otherwise extricate themselves. Through death, one could cleanse oneself of misdeeds committed and vindicate the social order that had been violated.

There is in suicide, it is true, an element of outright rebellion against the society that has caused the individual's failure. Lovers' suicide protests class inequality or the conservatism of the marriage institution which prevents the consummation of the couple's love. A student who fails protests, with suicide, against teachers, family, or friends; a corrupt employee, against employers; and parents who kill themselves along with their children, against the society that has not enabled them to live honorably. But though the act of suicide is by nature a protest, the Japanese tend to look upon it with a forgiving eye. Perhaps because suicide victims turn their anger not upon society, but upon themselves, they end up sanctioning, when all is said and done, the status quo.

To return to the discussion of the samurai's attitude toward death, especially as this attitude had developed by and during the Edo period (1600–1867), a work known as *Hagakure* (Hidden by leaves, *c*. 1716) is mentioned. This is a collection of heroic adventures and sayings gathered over many years by the scholar and poet Yamamoto Tsunetomo (1659–1719). In the author's view—perhaps the most extreme expression of this attitude—the key feature in the way of the samurai is his ability to die. The samurai, says Yamamoto, ought to "die like a madman": if once he lets even the shadow of common sense enter his consciousness, he will choose to live and will be unable to sacrifice his life for his lord "with a pure spirit." The doctrine of dying like a madman deviates even from the most extreme teaching of Confucianism, whose motivation for devotion to the family or the clan is the wish to base the social order, however conservative it may be, on foundations of reason. *Hagakure* seemed too radical even for Japan's feudal rulers, who banned it several times.

The same spirit of uncompromising fanaticism that appears in the life histories and death poems of samurai near the end of the Edo period can be felt among the monarchists and nationalists of the late nineteenth and early twentieth centuries. Indeed, during the decades prior to World War II, such extremists held the words of *Hagakure* to be the purest expression of loyalty to the emperor. The fanatic acts of suicide committed by the best of Japan's young men—crashing planes loaded with bombs into Allied warships—in a sense merely continued the samurai tradition of dying for one's ruler. Many of the youths undoubtedly believed they would win eternal life in Buddhist or Shinto fashion, but it was not this that motivated them so much as doing their duty to their fatherland and their emperor. They saw no point in living on in a world where their godlike ruler had been defeated.

Much of the responsibility for their deaths (the authorities knew even before the missions set out that Japan's fate in the war was sealed) must go to the Japanese government's propaganda machine, which produced books, including children's books and textbooks, containing stories about warriors dying a martyr's death and quoting death poems of bravery and resignation to fate. (The youths who died in suicide units often left death poems, as did most of the officers of the Japanese army.) I shall quote only one example from the many pieces of propaganda of the day. Toward the end of the war, a government publishing house issued a book entitled *Nihon-*

jin no Shiseikan (The view of the Japanese of life and death).[3]
The author, a professor in a government university and pre-
viously a member of the Foreign Office, presents accounts
of warriors' deaths from the history and literature of Japan,
some of which exceed the bounds of good taste. For example,
in the chapter on "Life and Death as Perceived by Japanese
Parents," the author quotes a ballad from the eighteenth
century that tells of a young warrior who falls in battle for
his lord. The youth's father turns to the weeping mother
and says, "Be happy, woman! Your son has died for a good
cause." "Thus," continues the author, "should a Japanese
father behave when his beloved son dies for the emperor."

It is perhaps no great wonder that the attitude of the samu-
rai (and the suicide pilot) has received more attention than
other views of death found in Japan. It should be remembered,
however, that this attitude has been only one influence in the
"typical" Japanese view of dying.

EARLY DEATH POEMS

Historically, most death poems have been in tanka form,
those composed by the court nobility refined and delicate,
and those by warriors more "masculine," often reflecting
feelings of intense loyalty to the feudal lord or the nation.
Later, Chinese death poems were written by Buddhist monks
and priests, by scholars of Chinese literature, and to a fair
extent by samurai. Death poems in haiku form, appearing
first in the sixteenth century, have been written by Japanese
from all levels of society. The writing of death poems as a
widespread practice, however, began during the Meiji period
(1868–1912).

Poems written just before death appear in the most ancient Japanese sources, including the *Kojiki,* the *Man'yoshu,* and the *Kokinshu.* The earliest example of a death poem seems to be that of Yamato Takeru-no-Mikoto, the hero of the *Kojiki* who turned into a white bird upon his death. Fatigued by adventures of conquest against various gods, he falls to his deathbed; realizing the malady is fatal, he sings:

The sabre-sword	*Otome no*
which I placed	*toko-no-be ni*
at the maiden's bed-side,	*waga okishi*
alas!	*tsurugi no tachi*
that sword!	*sono tachi wa ya*

"As soon as he had finished singing," says the text, "he died."[4] Previous chapters tell how the sword had been found inside the tail of a dragon, and how Yamato Takeru-no-Mikoto had left it in the house of Miyazuhime-no-Mikoto, who later became his wife. The exact meaning of the song is unclear. Is the hero lamenting the loss of the sword, a sacred symbol of Japan's imperial house? Or does his grief stem from having to part with his loved one?

Some of the tanka in the *Man'yoshu,* several of which are translated below, are more distinctly death poems. One is that of Kakinomoto-no-Hitomaro, who lived near the end of the seventh century or the beginning of the eighth. Though Hitomaro is considered the best of the poets whose works appear in the *Man'yoshu,* and though the Japanese style him "the father of Japanese poetry," little is known about his life. A nobleman, he served two emperors in various posts, but his principal role seems to have been that of court poet.

He accompanied the emperor on journeys of state and composed laudatory poems in his honor. In addition to those dedicated to the emperor and his retinue, he wrote poems about parting, grief, journeys, love, and the like. The tanka known as his death poem bears the title "In Iwami Province, About to Die." The woman of the poem is perhaps one of his wives, Yosami-no-Otome, herself a poet.

Not knowing	*Kamo-yama no*
that my body lies	*iwane shi makeru*
upon Mount Kamo's rocks,	*ware o kamo*
my love	*shirani to imo ga*
awaits me.	*machitsutsu aruramu*

The power struggles of the time often brought men of the imperial family to a tragic end. Prince Arima (640–58), for instance, was sentenced to death for alleged treason. On the way to Iwashiro (Wakayama Prefecture), where he was executed, Arima ties two pine boughs together and sings, as recorded in the *Man'yoshu*:

If fate agrees	*Iwashiro no*
I shall return	*hamamatsu ga e o*
to Iwashiro's coast	*hikimusubi*
and see the pine boughs	*masakiku araba*
I united.	*mata kaerimimu*

A similar fate overtook Prince Otsu (663–86), the third son of Emperor Temmu (d. 686) and second in line to the throne. When his father died, Otsu was accused, apparently unjustly, of conspiring to the throne, and was sentenced to death.

Otsu had a reputation for nobility of character, and his execution caused great sorrow among his contemporaries. More than anything he did while alive, however, it was the poem he said before his death that won him his place in history:

This is the last day	*Momozutau*
I shall see the mallards	*Iware-no-ike ni*
crying over Lake Iware.	*naku kamo o*
Then shall I disappear	*kyō nomi mite ya*
into the clouds.	*kumogakurinamu*

In the early part of the Heian period, as new Buddhist sects arose in Japan with the return from China of students of Buddhism, life began to be depicted in poetry as an ephemeral illusion. Here is a poem of Minamoto-no-Shitago (911–83), a nobleman, a scholar, and one of his age's foremost poets:

This world—	*Yononaka o*
to what may I liken it?	*nani ni tatoemu*
To autumn fields	*aki no ta o*
lit dimly in the dusk	*honoka ni terasu*
by lightning flashes.	*yoi no inazuma*

It was the flower, however, that came to be the principal symbol of the fleetingness of man's existence. Death was not referred to by means of a corpse, but was likened to wilting flower petals. The short-lived blossom represents the powerlessness of life before death and the delusion in our aspiration to live forever. Yet the flower also symbolizes beauty. Japanese poetry regards the world through the change of seasons with longing and sorrow—longing for the renewal of spring after fall and winter, and sorrow that the blossoming cherries should last so short a time. It is natural, then, that the death poems of the Heian period are strewn with images of flowers.

The following story appears in the *Heike Monogatari* (The tale of the Heike), a collection of stories about heroic warriors written in the latter half of the twelfth century. Taira-no-Tadanori (1144–84) was in command of the western flank of the army of the Heike (Taira) clan when Okabe Tadazumi, a warrior of the Genji (Minamoto) clan, overtook him on the battlefield. Tadazumi galloped alongside Tadanori and grappled with him. Tadanori, however, overpowered Tadazumi and was about to cut off his head when one of Tadazumi's retainers drew his sword and cut off Tadanori's right arm. Tadanori pushed Tadazumi aside and said, "Stay away from me! I wish to say the death prayer!" He turned toward the west and chanted a Buddhist prayer. Then Tadazumi approached him from behind and beheaded him. Tadanori's death poem, which he carried with him into battle as was the way among warriors, was found fasted to his quiver. The poem is entitled "A Flower at a Traveler's Inn":

Overtaken by darkness
I will lodge under
the boughs of a tree.
Flowers alone
host me tonight.

Yukikurete
ko-no-shita kage o
yado toseba
hana ya koyoi no
aruji naramashi

The same epic tells the story of Minamoto-no-Yorimasa (1104–80), a nobleman and general who served eight emperors. He is famous as the soldier-hero who defeated a monstrous bird that threatened the imperial palace; he is also considered one of the best poets of his time. The army of the Genji clan, which Yorimasa led, was defeated in a great battle, and Yorimasa, wounded by an arrow in his knee, decided to kill himself. He summoned his retainer Tonau and ordered him to strike off his head, but Tonau wept bitterly and refused to do so. Yorimasa turned to the west, chanted, "I put my trust in Amida Buddha," and spoke these words:

Like a rotten log	*Umoregi no*
half-buried in the ground—	*hana saku koto mo*
my life, which	*nakarishi ni*
has not flowered, comes	*mi no naru hate zo*
to this sad end.	*kanashikarikeru*

Then he pierced his sword deep into his abdomen and died. Weeping, Tonau cut off his master's head and, lest it fall into the hands of the victorious enemy, sank it in the river.

A flower image appears as well in the death poem of Saigyo (1118–90), one of Japan's most famous tanka poets. A warrior and a nobleman, Saigyo became a Buddhist monk at the age of twenty-nine. He was a leading figure in the poetic circles of his time, and his style greatly influenced Basho, who lived five centuries later. Saigyo's death poem presents a scene during the second lunar month, when cherry trees blossom and memorial services for the Buddha's death are held:

I wish to die	*Negawaku wa*
in spring, beneath	*hana no shita nite*
the cherry blossoms,	*haru shinamu*
while the springtime moon	*sono kisaragi no*
is full.	*mochizuki no koro*

DEATH POEMS OF SAMURAI

While early warriors expressed their view of the ephemeral world in terms of flowers, the death poems of the samurai of the Kamakura period and later employ a rather different vocabulary, influenced to a great extent by Zen Buddhism. Most samurai of the time lived and died by the sword, differing in this respect from Zen monks. But many of their death poems are Chinese poems, similar in form and content to those written by Zen monks. To illustrate, there follow four stories from the *Taiheiki* (Chronicle of grand pacification), an anthology of heroic adventure stories with historical references, probably compiled in the middle of the fourteenth century.

> Toshimoto took out of his robe a scroll of paper and, after wiping his neck with it, spread it out and wrote his death poem:
>
> > From ancient times the saying comes,
> > "There is no death; there is no life."
> > Indeed, the skies are cloudless
> > And the river waters clear.*
>
> Toshimoto then laid down his brush and smoothed his hair with his hand. At that very moment, the blade of

* Because Chinese poems are written series of Chinese characters, many characters homophonous with each other, to render the poems in romanized form would provide little clue to the content of the original. These poems, therefore, are given in translation only.

the sword flashed behind him; his head fell forward and his body followed, covering the head.

* * * *

Suketomo sat upright on an animal pelt and wrote a farewell poem in praise of Buddhist truth:

> All five manners* of my fleeting form
> And its four elements† return to naught—
> I put my neck to the unsheathed sword.
> Its cut is but a breath of wind.

He wrote the date, signed his name, and laid the brush beside him. Then the executioner approached from behind, and Suketomo's head fell forward onto the animal pelt, his body still holding itself upright.

* * * *

Minamoto-no-Tomoyuki sat upright on an animal pelt, took out his inkstone, and calmly wrote his death poem:

> For two and forty years
> I wavered between life and death.
> Now hills and rivers overturn.
> The earth and sky return to nothingness.

Beneath the poem he wrote, "The nineteenth of the tenth month," and signed his name; then he put his brush aside, crossed his arms, and straightened his back.

---

* five manners: bodily form, feelings, senses, impulses, and consciousness.

† four elements: earth, water, air, and fire.

The executioner came around behind him and in an instant his severed head fell forward.

* * * *

[Shiaku Sho'on was a monk at the time of his death, though he was, by origin, a samurai. After the defeat of his lord's army, he preferred to die as a warrior rather than retire, as a monk would have done, from "the vanity of this world." His eldest son having already committed suicide, the younger son, Shiro, requests to do likewise. Shiaku stops him and says:]

"Wait a while. It is not proper that a son should die before his father. When I am dead, you, too, may die." Shiro sheathed his dagger and knelt before his father, who looked down on him and laughed approvingly. Then Shiaku ordered that a monk's stool be put near the middle gate and sat upon it cross-legged. He took out his inkstone and wrote his death poem:

> The sharp-edged sword, unsheathed,
> Cuts through the void—
> Within the raging fire
> A cool wind blows.

He then folded his arms, bent his head forward, and ordered: "Strike!" Shiro, stripped to the waist, struck off his father's head; then setting his sword upright, he thrust it to the hilt into his own stomach and fell forward on his face, dead. Three retainers who had been watching ran forward and threw themselves on the same blade, falling with their heads together like fish on a skewer.

Such are the stories of *seppuku* as they appear in one account, although we must not forget, of course, the alterations made when the event is described in folklore and literature.

In addition to poems in the Chinese tradition, warriors also wrote tanka death poems. Many of these poems, too, are tinged with the spirit of Buddhism.

Ota Dokan (1432–86), a scholar of military arts and a poet, was stabbed as he was bathing. Clutching the dagger that pierced his body, he uttered the following tanka and died:

Had I not known	*Kakaru toki*
that I was dead	*sa koso inochi no*
already	*oshikarame*
I would have mourned	*kanete nakimi to*
my loss of life.	*omoishirazuba*

Chikamasa was a pupil of the well-known master Ikkyu Sojun (1394–1481). According to folklore, Chikamasa was greeted at the hour of his death by the three Buddhas of the past, the present, and the future, riding on purple clouds with twenty-five escorts. Chikamasa first ordered his son to bring him his weapons, then shot an arrow at the Buddha in the center. The warrior thus showed his contempt for the celestial retinue and his unconcern for the world to come. Before his death, Chikamasa said this poem:

One day you are born	*Umarenuru*
you die the next—	*sono akatsuki ni*
today,	*shininureba*
at twilight,	*kyō no yūbe wa*
autumn breezes blow.	*akikaze zo fuku*

Ouchi Yoshitaka (1507–51) was a samurai general and ruler of most of the island of Kyushu. He was a man of good character who developed commercial relations with China and Korea, and his domain became a center of liberal culture in which warriors and noblemen from other regions sought refuge. It is said that he met twice with the leader of the first Jesuit missionaries to Japan, St. Francis Xavier, and even allowed him to preach in his province. In 1551 one of his generals rebelled and overpowered his army. Before committing suicide, Yoshitaka composed a death poem, the last lines of which are taken from a Chinese translation of the Buddhist scripture *Kongo-gyo* (Diamond sutra), which teaches that the essence of all is void:

Both the victor	*Utsu hito mo*
and the vanquished are	*utaruru hito mo*
but drops of dew,	*morotomo ni*
but bolts of lightning—	*nyo ro yaku nyo den*
thus should we view the world.	*ō sa ni ze kan*

But not all death poems of this war-torn period, from the middle of the fifteenth to the end of the sixteenth centuries, were written in a Buddhist mood. Many warriors left to the world hearts burning with fanatic loyalty to their clan, and this fanaticism often overshadowed any religious spirit.

A warrior called Akaboshi was a vassal to Ryuzoji Takanobu (1529–84). The latter suspected Akaboshi of wishing to rebel against him and so took two of his children, a girl of eight years and a boy whose age is not given, as hostages. Takanobu eventually crucified them. The soldier in charge of the execution turned the children westward (toward paradise), his eyes brimming with tears. Before dying, the boy, Shinroku, asked, "Where is my homeland?" "Toward the east," answered the soldier, whereupon the child replied with this poem:

Please don't face me	*Waga omote*
toward the west	*nishi ni na mukeso*
lest I should turn	*Akaboshi no*
my back upon my father,	*oya ni ushiro o*
Akaboshi.	*miseji to omoeba*

Another warrior by the name of Takemata Hideshige lost a battle to his rival, Shibata Katsuie (1522–83). Before dying, he said:

Shall Ashura*	*Ashura-ō ni*
subdue a man like me?	*ware o torameya*
I shall be born again	*yagate mata*
and then I'll cut the head	*umarete toramu*
off Katsuie . . .	*Katsuie ga kubi*

Yoshida Shoin (1830–59) was a nationalist thinker and educator. Born into a samurai family, he was later adopted by his uncle, a teacher in the art of warfare. It is said of Yoshida that at the age of nine he was already lecturing to the ruler of his province on military arts. While in his twenties, he came under the influence of dissidents to the rule of the

---

* Ashura: in Brahmanism and Hinduism, a mythological demon who thirsts for battle and fights for the gods. In Buddhist folklore, he becomes a kind of war god.

shogun, whose government consequently stripped him of the rank of samurai and ceased paying him the concomitant stipend. After some time he was pardoned, but in 1854 he was caught attempting to escape from Japan in a ship from the American fleet, apparently with the intention of studying Western warfare. He was sentenced to confinement on the grounds of his house and spent the remaining five years of his life writing and teaching. He demanded that foreigners be banned from the country and that the emperor be reinstated; his followers later played an important role in the Meiji Restoration of 1868. Motivated by his hatred for the shogun's regime and his nationalistic zeal, he formed a plan to assassinate a high government official. The conspiracy, however, was discovered by the government, and Yoshida was executed in 1859 at the age of only twenty-nine. When his sentence was announced about a week before his execution, he wrote a poem to his parents expressing his deepest respect for them in the best tradition of Confucianism. His death poem, however, he dedicated to the emperor:

> Though my corpse rot
> beneath the ground
> of Musashi,*
> my soul remains forever
> Japanese.

> *Mi wa tatoi*
> *Musashi no nobe ni*
> *kuchinu tomo*
> *todome okamashi*
> *yamato-damashii*

The poet Nomura Boto (1806–67) wrote a death poem in a similar vein. She too was born into a samurai family and was

---

* Musashi: the province comprising present-day Saitama and Tokyo prefectures.

a supporter of the emperor. After the death of her husband she had shaved her head and become a Buddhist nun. In spite of this she cast her lot with the monarchists and was exiled by the shogunal government.

Though moss	*Kazu naranu*
will overgrow	*kono mi wa koke ni*
my useless corpse,	*umorete mo*
the seeds of patriotism	*yamato-gokoro no*
shall ne'er decay.	*tane wa kuchisezu*

The life story of Nogi Maresuke (1849–1912) reflects, more than any other, the spirit of the Japanese warrior. Born into the nobility, Nogi became a high-ranking army official. In 1877, while he was leading a battalion, his unit's insignia were captured by forces hostile to the government, and Nogi prepared for suicide. Those around him prevented him from killing himself, but shame for the defeat never left him as long as he lived. In 1894, during the Sino-Japanese War, he was in charge of the division that captured Port Arthur in a single day; later he became the governor of Taiwan. During the Russo-Japanese War of 1904, he fought many a bloody battle as a general. This war, in which he himself lost two sons, left him with a deep sense of guilt at the loss of so many soldiers. After the war he was awarded with a high title of nobility and was appointed as a military adviser to the government. Emperor Meiji himself thought highly of him and entrusted him with the education of the sons of court nobility. Nogi was much admired for his firm moral principles, and to many he epitomized the Japanese warrior. When the emperor died in 1912, Nogi felt that life had lost its meaning, and he committed suicide, together with his wife, on the day of the emperor's funeral. Thus, as he states in his death poem, Nogi fulfilled the ancient obligation of the warrior not to remain in the world after his lord has left it:

The Master of the World	*Utsushiyo o*
has passed away—	*kami sarishi mama*
and after him,	*ōkimi no*
eager to serve my lord,	*miato shitaite*
go I.	*ware wa yuku nari*

I will close this section with the death poem of Fujita Koshiro (1842–65), a samurai who supported the emperor in the Meiji Restoration. He fought against the shogun's forces, but his army was defeated and he was condemned to death. Though his death poem reveals his fanaticism, its stringency is softened by an image from nature in the traditional style of love poetry:

Plum petals	*Saku ume wa*
falling in the wind	*kaze ni hakanaku*
leave aromatic odors	*chiru totemo*
on the sleeve	*nioi wa kimi ga*
of the imperial robe.	*sode ni utsushite*

DEATH POEMS OF LOVERS

We learn from Japanese history and literature that loyalty to death was not confined only to warriors. The intensity of emotion displayed by samurai toward their lords was matched by the loyalty of Japanese women for the men they loved;

indeed, the idea of "love consummated in death" is present in the earliest written sources. One of the stories in the *Kojiki* concerns the heir-apparent to the throne, Karu-no-Mikoto, and his sister Karu-no-Iratsume. Just before his succession, the crown prince seduces his sister, singing a stormy and sensual song. Their forbidden love must have incurred the anger of the entire nation, for the text says that "all the officials and likewise the people of the Empire turned against the Heir Apparent Karu."[5] Karu-no-Mikoto is banished; he goes into exile singing love songs. His sister, unable to restrain her love, sets out after him, singing a love song of her own. The lovers meet, exchange more songs, and commit suicide.

These two are the first in a long line of lovers' suicides in Japanese history and folklore. In the *Harima Fudoki* (Topographical record of Harima,* c. 713), we find the story of the goddess Awami who pursues her lover, the god Hanami, to the edge of a marsh. When she does not find him there, her distress overwhelms her and she "takes a dagger, pierces her stomach, and falls into the marsh." The story is told, apparently, as an explanation of the place name—Harasaki-numa, "marsh of the split stomach." This is also the first mention in Japanese literature of suicide by *seppuku*.

The *Kojiki* contains the first death poem sung by a woman. The poem is that of Oto-Tachibana, who dies for her lover, Yamato Takeru-no-Mikoto, whose own death poem is quoted above. Yamato Takeru-no-Mikoto is nearly burned to death in a field fire lit by his enemy, the ruler of Sagamu (or Sagami, part of present-day Kanagawa Prefecture). He escapes, however, and continues his adventures. Just as he and his retinue

* Harima: the southern part of present-day Hyogo Prefecutre.

are about to cross the sea, "the deity of that crossing" stirs up the waves. Oto-Tachibana offers to sacrifice her life to appease the god. The men on the boat take many sedge mats, skin rugs, and silk carpets and set them upon the waves. Oto-Tachibana seats herself on top of them, whereupon the waves subside. The ship then sets sail, and the abandoned woman sings:

Ah! thou [whom I] enquired of,	*Sanesashi*
standing in the midst	*Sagamu no ono ni*
of the flames of the fire	*moyuru hi no*
burning on the little moor of Sagamu,	*honoka ni tachite*
where the true peak pierces![6]	*toishi kimi wa mo*

Seven days later Oto-Tachibana's comb drifts ashore. A mausoleum is erected and the comb is placed in it.

The literature of the Heian period, written largely by ladies of the court, contains not only light stories of romance, but tragic tales of love ending in death. One of the literary creations of the period is the *Ise Monogatari* (Tales of Ise), a chain of stories interwoven with more than two hundred tanka, most of them about love among the court nobility of the tenth century. One story tells of a man who lives in the provinces but goes to the capital to join the service of a nobleman, parting from his wife with great emotion. Three years pass during which the wife hears nothing from her husband. Unable to wait for him any longer, she at last gives in to a persistent suitor, but on the first night they spend together, her husband turns up without warning and knocks on the portals of the house. The woman, without opening the gate, passes a poem to her husband in a note, confessing that, "grown weary of waiting for three long years," she is sharing her bed for the first time with another man. Her husband sends back a poem of his own, hoping that "she will love her new man as much as she loved him." Before he goes, he receives another note from his wife declaring that "although others have sought her love, her heart belongs to him alone." The husband, however, turns his back on her and leaves. She pursues him but fails to overtake him, giving up the chase beside a clear-running stream. Before dying, she writes her last poem on a rock beside the brook with blood drawn from her finger:

The man I loved	*Aiomowade*
refused to hear	*karenuru hito o*
my pleadings—	*todomekane*
he abandoned me and now	*wagami wa ima zo*
my life fades away.	*kiehatenumeru*

Among the many fascinating stories in the *Genji Monogatari,* there appears the tale of the girl Ukifune. It is not clear whom she loves, but at least two young men are enamored of her. In a way characteristic of the Japanese, Ukifune decides to do away with herself in order to solve her dilemma. Just before throwing herself into the Uji River, she writes a number of poems. She sends the following, her last, to Prince Niou, the more insistent of her suitors:

If I leave	*Kara o dani*
no trace behind	*ukiyo no naka ni*
in this fleeting world	*todomezuba*
what then could you	*izuku o haka to*
reproach?	*kimi mo uramin*

Ukifune is pulled from the river and saved, but she shaves her head and abandons the world for the monastery.

Another woman who left such a poem, and who did succeed in drowning herself, was the mistress of the nobleman Fujiwara-no-Moronaga (1138–92). Moronaga, who lived with his mistress only while in his home province, was about to return to the city of Kyoto, where the provincial nobility spent the greater part of every year. Before returning he gave her a *biwa,* a stringed instrument similiar to the mandolin, as a present. Unable to bear the sorrow of parting from her lover, she threw herself into a river after composing the following poem:

Thus say unto him,	*Yotsu-no-o no*
"She whose life hung	*shirabe ni kakete*
on the *biwa* melody	*Mitsuse-gawa*
has sunk beneath the waters	*shizumi hateshi to*
of the Mitsuse."*	*kimi ni tsutaeyo*[7]

During the civil wars of the fourteenth to the sixteenth centuries, the fate of many warriors' wives was no brighter than that of their husbands when the latter suffered defeat in battle. In the *Taiheiki,* we find the story of Sakai Sadatoshi and his wife. Sadatoshi is exiled from his home, and while wandering dispiritedly throughout the country, he is eventually apprehended by enemies and condemned to die. He does not shrink from death, but before his execution, he is grieved not to know what has become of his wife and children.

---

* Mitsuse (River): a name for the counterpart in Japanese folklore of the River Styx.

He asks the guard to return the dagger he had always kept on his person and entrusts it to a monk, who agrees to deliver the dagger to Sadatoshi's loved ones. At this, Sadatoshi is content; he sits straight up on the animal skin and recites this poem:

When luck held out	*Mina hito no*
and others thrived	*yo ni aru toki wa*
I counted not at all—	*kazu narade*
but when disaster falls	*uki ni wa morenu*
we share one fate.	*wagami narikeri*

He then calls Buddha's name ten times and submits calmly to the executioner's blow. The monk takes up the dagger and the robe in which Sadatoshi died and goes to Kamakura, where he finds Sadatoshi's wife and gives her the articles. She falls weeping to the floor, unable to bear her grief; she then brings out her inkstone and writes this poem on the hem of her husband's robe:

For whose eyes	*Tare miyo to*
did he send	*katami o hito no*
these things?	*todomeken*
How could I live	*taete aru beki*
and bear so great a grief?	*inochi naranu ni*

Covering her head with the gown, she thrusts the dagger into her breast and dies.

The following war story is found in the chronicles of a samurai family of the fifteenth or sixteenth century. The general of a certain fortress escapes from his enemy into the

confines of a Buddhist temple. One of the gen
rebels against him and attacks the temple. The ge..
mits suicide by *seppuku*. His retainer, a warrior named h,
go, strikes off his head with a "mercy blow" and kills himself
as well. Hyogo's son dies in the same battle. Hyogo's wife,
upon hearing of her son's and husband's deaths, broke into
bitter tears and died within two days. She left this poem:

They who are no more	*Aru wa naku*
increase from day to day—	*naki wa kazusō*
in such a world	*yononaka mo*
how could I think	*wagami no ue to*
that when it came to me . . .	*omowazarishi o*

The wars of the samurai in the sixteenth century, in which
many thousands of women lost their husbands and sons,
sometimes caused strange and tragic complications. Nara
Yayoi, the sister of Nara Sakon, a samurai, was loved and
courted for a number of years by another samurai, Sadamitsu.
Sakon, however, disliked Sadamitsu and refused to allow the
two to marry. In the course of time Sakon and Sadamitsu
found themselves in opposing camps, and Sakon was killed
with an arrow shot by Sadamitsu. Yayoi was captured and
married to Sadamitsu. She pretended to resign herself to the
marriage, but secretly wrote a last letter, with her death poem,
to her mother. After sending the letter, she stole Sadamitsu's
sword and killed first him, then herself. In refusing to share
a bed with her brother's killer she proved her loyalty to her
family—but is the reader mistaken to hear a note of love for
Sadamitsu in her death poem?

My heart   *Omoigawa*
is a bottomless river,   *fukaki fuchise wa*
a raging torrent—   *hayakeredo*
how can I throw my name   *sasou mizu ni wa*
into the tempting waters?   *na o nagasameya*

During the Edo period, the Japanese witnessed another way of life developing alongside that of the effeminate nobility and severely masculine samurai—that of merchants and artisans in Edo (present-day Tokyo), Osaka, and Kyoto. Historians sometimes call this era "the roaring Edo period," for the inhabitants of Edo, the capital, were known for carefree living. Theaters in the city staged romantic plays featuring "love as strong as death," and occasional incidents of lovers' suicide would become the talk of the day. The account of one such incident follows:

Not long ago [perhaps in the middle of the eighteenth century], in a geisha house named Kariganeya in Edo's red-light district, the Yoshiwara, there lived a geisha named Uneme. A Buddhist monk fell in love with her and used to visit her frequently. The proprietress of the house did not look kindly on their affair and employed various ruses to keep the two from meeting. The monk, unable to bear their separation, killed himself. When Uneme heard the news of his death, she escaped from her house and threw herself into Kagami-ga-ike [lit., mirror lake]. Her death poem alludes to another Uneme*

* The story of the earlier Uneme (a common name for courtesans) appears in the *Man'yoshu*.

who, about a thousand years before, had drowned herself in Sarusawa-no-ike [lit., monkey-brook lake, in Nara]:

If you know not	*Na o sore to*
who I am, hear:	*shirazu tomo shire*
Like the one who cast herself	*Sarusawa no*
into the Lake of Monkeys	*ato o Kagami-ga-*
I drown myself in Mirror Lake.	*ike ni shizumeba*[8]

In many of the death poems written by Japanese women, the reader may sense a longing for a place of refuge from the many hardships the women encounter. The following death poem belongs to a woman named Oroku and dates from the first part of the seventeenth century. Oroku marries a certain Sakon, the retainer of a provincial ruler, and bears him a male child. She is treated cruelly by her mother-in-law, however, and finally kills herself. This poem appears in her will:

And had my days been longer	*Nagaraete*
still the darkness	*kono yo no yami wa*
would not leave this world—	*yomo hareji*
along death's path, among the hills	*shide no yamaji no*
I shall behold the moon.	*iza tsuki o min*[9]

The moon symbolizes salvation in the world beyond from the sufferings of the present life.

DEATH POEMS AND ZEN BUDDHISM

At the moment of death, say followers of the Jodo sects

of Buddhism, the dying person is greeted either by Amida, the Buddha of Everlasting Light, or by Kannon, the Bodhisattva of Compassion and Love. Anyone who calls the name of Buddha before dying is reborn in the Pure Land in the West. We find in religious literature the description of terrible afflictions that befall the wicked after death, but most accounts depict such hells as temporary states in which even saints may be found, saving others from torture. All such beliefs are defined as *tariki,* "[salvation through] power from without," as opposed to *jiriki,* "[salvation through] power from within." Although most Japanese Buddhists belong to the Jodo sects, the belief that salvation comes through inner enlightenment, a tenet of Zen Buddhism, has always been strong among the well educated.

There is a trend in the "inner enlightenment" sects toward voluntary death. Kukai (774–835), known posthumously as Kobo Daishi, was a learned Buddhist monk who sailed to China to study the mysteries of the Shingon sect. On his return to Japan, he founded a large Buddhist temple on Mount Koya (Wakayama Prefecture) and spread the esoteric doctrine of Buddhism among noblemen and peasants alike. It is said that Kukai died by fasting till the skin stuck to his bones.

Buddhist literature reports that Eisai (1141–1215), one of the founders of Japanese Zen, knew just when his death was approaching. He journeyed to Kyoto in order to "show people how to die." Upon his arrival, he first preached to the crowd, then sat completely still in the upright Zen position, and died. However, when his followers complained that his death had been too sudden, he revived. He died for good in the same manner five days later. His pupil Eicho

(d. 1247) anticipated his own death and met it sitting up-
right; other famous monks died in the same way.[10]

Stories about dying at will are not told exclusively about
monks. A nineteenth-century samurai scholar relates, for
instance, the story of the death of a poet named Hasegawa
Shume (*c.* 1700). Shume wrote before dying:

Throughout the frosty night	*Okiakasu*
I lay awake. When morning bells	*shimoyo no kane ni*
rang out, my heart grew clear—	*kokoro sumu*
upon this fleeting dream-world	*ukiyo no yume no*
dawn is waking.	*akegata no sora*

"When he had spoken these words," says the text, "his
breathing grew shallow. Those pressing around him urged,
'Call Buddha's name.' But Shume, rather than praying,
merely repeated aloud, 'Thanks, thanks.' Then he covered
himself and told them not to take away the blanket until a
certain hour. At the specified time, they drew back the cover
and found him dead."[11]

It is, however, the dying person's state of mind, rather
than the ability to control the manner of dying, to which
importance is attached among followers of the "inner en-
lightenment" sects. One who dies lusting for life in this world
or for salvation in the next is not enlightened. This is why
many death poems express not only resignation to death,
but even indifference to the prospects of a world beyond.
Indeed, such attitudes gave rise to a rejection of the very act
of writing death poems, a subject discussed below. Enlighten-
ment as understood by Zen Buddhists does not confer un-
derstanding beyond that possessed by ordinary people but

is rather a state in which consciousness is free from any theoretical thinking. "When a simple man gains knowledge," says Zen scripture, "he is wise. When a wise man gains understanding, he is simple."

The identification of enlightenment with a state of natural simplicity—which extends even until one's dying moments—originates in ancient Taoist philosophy, which reached Japan during the eighth century and which influenced Japanese Zen Buddhism no less than Indian Buddhism did. Alongside the gloomy vision of the world as a fleeting illusion, traces can be felt of the Taoist philosophy of the forgetfulness of self being the essence of wholeness and purity. The writings of the philosophers Lao-tzu (sixth cent. B.C.) and Chuang-tzu (third cent. B.C.) do not so much teach how to *think* as how to *be*. When the world behaves according to its nature, say the Taoist sages, everything finds its place of its own accord. It is when one forces principles on the world that one interferes with its natural workings. Sunflowers manage to grow without the farmer pulling on their stalks every morning, and so it is with man. He need not ask himself about every step he takes, wondering by what principles he ought to conduct himself. Taoists define correct behavior as "nonaction" (Ch., *wu wei;* J., *mui*), which does not mean "sit still and do nothing." Rather, it refers to action in which natural processes are not interfered with—actions as natural as the growth of sunflowers. "The wise man," says Chuang-tzu, "walks by the light of chaos, the light of darkness. He does not impose distinctions, but leaves everything in its place. This is clarity of mind."

In one of Chuang-tzu's stories, he describes the death of sages who knew the secret of the Tao, the Way:

The four sages Szu, Y

each other. They sai

head, Life as his bac

knows Life and Deat

be one of us." The f

There was no barri

Not long after

and asked how h

of the master is detor...

as a hunchback's and my organs

My chin sticks in my navel, my shoulders rise

my head and my pigtail points to the sky. The elements of nature must be all confused." His heart was calm and his manner carefree. He limped to the well, looked at his reflection in the water and said, "My, my! How the Maker of Things is deforming me!" Szu asked, "Does this upset you?" "Why should it?" said Yü. "If my left arm becomes a rooster, I will herald the dawn. If my right arm becomes a crossbow, I'll shoot down a bird and roast it. If my buttocks turn into wheels and my spirit into a horse, I'll go for a ride. What need will I have for a carriage? I was born when it was time to be born, and I shall die when it is time to die. If we are in peace with time and follow the order of things, neither sorrow nor joy will move us. The ancients called this 'freedom from bondage.' Those who are entangled with the appearance of things cannot free themselves. But nothing can overcome the order of nature. Why should I be upset?"

Shortly afterward, Lai fell ill. He lay gasping on the verge of death. His wife and children were gathered

, weeping. Li, who had come to see him,
! Be off with you! Do not distrub the change!"
e leaned back on the door and said to Lai, "Great
e Maker of Things! What will become of you now?
here will he send you? Will you be the liver of a rat
or the leg of an insect?" Lai said, "A child who obeys
his father and mother will go wherever they tell him
to go—east, west, south, or north. Yin and yang, the
elements of nature, are they not to a man like father and
mother? If I were not to obey them now that they have
brought me to the point of death, how wayward I should
be! They are not to be blamed. The great earth burdens
me with a body, forces upon me the toil of life, eases
me in old age, and calms me in death. If life is good,
death is good also. If an ironsmith were casting metal
and the metal were to jump up and say, 'Make me into
the best of all swords!' the ironsmith would regard it
as a bad omen. Now that my human form is decompos-
ing, were I to say, 'I want to be a man! Nothing but
a man!' the Maker of Things would think me most
unworthy. Heaven and earth are a great forge and the
Maker of Things is a master ironsmith. Can the place
he is sending me to be the wrong place?"

When Chuang-tzu himself was about to die, his disciples
wished to prepare for him a lavish funeral. But Chuang-tzu
said that all the furnishings for his burial were already there:
heaven and earth for his coffin, the sun, the moon, and the
stars for ornaments, and the world of "ten thousand things"
for a parting gift. Still, his disciples insisted and argued that
unless he was properly buried, the fowl of the air would eat

his flesh. To this Chuang-tzu replied, "Above ground, vultures and crows will eat me. Below ground, crickets and ants will eat me. It does not seem fair to deprive the former just to feed the latter."

In addition to Taoist philosophy, Zen Buddhism has another important source in the Madhyamika, "middle path," school of Buddhism, founded by the Indian philosopher Nagarjuna, who lived in the second and third centuries A.D. It is unlikely that Nagarjuna had heard of the Chinese philosophers. By contrast with the colorful style of the latter, Nagarjuna writes in a concise, methodical manner, in a way that is typical of Indian thinkers. However, his doctrine of the "void" closely resembles Taoist philosophy.

Nagarjuna submits the idea of the mutual dependence of all things, a central principle of early Buddhist philosophy, to logical analysis and finds that because a "thing" can be defined only in relation to something else, no "thing" is absolutely identical to itself and therefore cannot exist as such. With this argument Nagarjuna refutes all possible descriptions of "reality." He does not deny its existence, but maintains only that we cannot think this reality, as our thoughts are confused and self-contradictory. Nagarjuna does not hesitate to attack even the Buddhist doctrine of doctrines—that of salvation from the "world of senses" in the absolute peace of nirvana. Salvation from the world of sorrow and pain is not to be attained by passing from a state of inferior being to a more exalted state, but by ceasing to think. Like the Taoists, Nagarjuna rejects the philosophical viewpoint entirely, seeing in it the origin of ignorance and suffering. With this attitude he solves the problem of death as well. When one understands that the distinction between life and death is as arbitrary and as illusory as all other distinctions, one finds the solution in the disappearance of the problem.

Both Taoist philosophers and Buddhists of the Madhyamika school, then, saw speculative thought about reality as the root of all evil. Likewise, from the very beginnings of Zen in the sixth century, no importance has been attached to rituals, to sacred writings, or to philosophical discussion. Such an anti-speculative attitude is apparent in thousands of Zen anecdotes from China and Japan, as the following sayings of Joshu (Chao-chou; 778–897), a Zen master from China, demonstrate:

> Someone asked, "When one is confronted with disaster, how can one avoid it?"
> Joshu said, "That's it!"
> (The disaster lies only in the consciousness of "disaster." When you are in a given situation but do not define it, it is not "good" or "bad"; you simply react according to the circumstances.)

> Someone asked, "What is my true nature?"
> Joshu said, "If that is what you say, what is it that you dislike?"
> (If you search for your "true" nature, you grant the existence of a "false" one. If you make no attempt to define your nature, you will find nothing in it that is not true.)

> Passing by the main hall, Joshu saw a monk worshiping. Joshu hit him once with his stick.

The monk said, "After all, worshiping is a good thing."

Joshu said, "A good thing isn't as good as nothing."[12]

Zen literature eventually came to serve as a means to en-lightenment in Zen monasteries. Several times a week, every monk would meet alone with the master. The latter would tell an anecdote or present a *koan,* a sort of problem or riddle from Zen literature. The monk's response would not neces-sarily be verbal, and it is often difficult to see the connection between the answer and the anecdote. Here is a dialogue between a Japanese master and monk from the end of the eighteenth or the beginning of the nineteenth century:

MASTER: Where will you go after death?
MONK: Excuse me for a minute. I have to go to the toilet.[13]

As in Zen anecdotes from China, the problem of death is treated as a pseudo-problem. The Zen master asks a trap question to see if the monk will display any metaphysical leanings. The monk, however, evading this aspect of the question and indicating thereby that he knows nothing of what will happen "after death," reacts only to "going" and demonstrates with the only kind of "going" known to him— moving from one concrete place to another.

In 1828, the Japanese poet Yamamoto Ryokan (1758–1831), himself a Zen monk, wrote to his friend a letter in the same vein as the sayings of Joshu, following an earthquake that killed thousands of people. He said, "When you suffer a calamity—then be it so; now is the time of calamity. When you die—then be it so; now is the time to die. Thus you save yourself from calamity and death."

It is not then to be wondered at, that in spite of the famous self-discipline of Zen monks, tradition often ascribes to them the simplest and most natural conduct just before their death. Such is the case with two of the central figures in Japanese Zen Buddhism, Ikkyu Sojun and Sengai Gibon (1750–1837), both of whose death poems appear in this anthology. There is, however, no evidence that they wrote the poems immediately before dying. Ikkyu, just before his death, protested, "I don't want to die!" Sengai was asked by one of his pupils if he had anything to say before passing away. He replied, "I don't want to die." His pupils, astounded to hear this, asked, "What was that you said?" "I really don't want to die," repeated Sengai. Both he and Ikkyu died at the age of eighty-eight. It is also reported of Sengai that a man once came to him and declared that he was disgusted with life. Sengai answered with a *kyoka,* a satirical tanka:

If your time to die has come	*Shini ni kite*
and you die—very well!	*shinu toki nareba—*
If your time to die has come	*shinu ga yoshi*
and you don't—	*shinisokonōte*
all the better!	*shinanu nao yoshi*

I was once told that a certain master of recent times exclaimed on his deathbed, "I don't want to die!" and burst out crying. When his pupils gathered around to wipe his tears, they saw that his eyes were completely dry. This man greeted death with a "natural" reaction, but perhaps wished to suggest that he was not bound even by "naturalness."

We find mention of the custom of writing death poems in a fifteenth-century book whose anonymous author states, "I don't know about China, but in our country Zen monks write death poetry. Most of them compose the poem while they are still healthy and pretend, when they die, to compose it on the spot. Some of these poems are nonsense; others are praiseworthy. But doesn't such a practice contradict the monks' withdrawal from society?"[14] An eighteenth-century scholar of literature makes the same point, adding an anecdote to sharpen it:

Zen monks ... usually write death poems. I know myself of two or three monks who composed theirs at the moment of death—a very difficult feat. They thought, perhaps, that they were doing it for their pupils, but if the way of nature is to be respected, such a practice is not at all becoming. I recently heard a story about a Zen priest from the town of Kizu who wanted to "die properly." He changed his clothes, wrote a death poem, and died sitting upright. The priest who took over his position in the temple was lying inside his mosquito net one summer day when all at once he saw the figure of a man. He looked more closely and discerned a tall priest. When he asked, "Who are you?" the figure replied, "I am the priest who lived here before you. At the hour of my death I paid so much attention to my appearance I am now having difficulty in crossing to the next world." The living priest prayed for the peace of his predecessor's spirit, and the figure hasn't come back since. ... The motive for striving so hard to write a death poem is the desire to impress others.[15]

Nishiyama Soin (1605–82), who was by all accounts a good poet, did not write a death poem at all. The probable reason has been recorded as follows:

> The poet Soin decided a long time before his death not to write a death poem. One day I heard him tell the story about a dying Buddhist priest. One of the priest's pupils came to his bed and said, "A man as famous for his learning and as gifted as you—surely you will write a death poem." The priest simply replied, "At an awesome time like this . . ." Then he closed his eyes and died. "How wonderful!" said Soin excitedly, repeating several times, "How wonderful!" For this reason I am sure that Soin, when he died, was taken up solely by the awesome meaning of his last moment.[16]

While some Zen monks were against the practice of writing death poems, we do find numerous examples of such poems in the literature. The fact that in Zen there was criticism of this custom is not surprising due to the abhorrence on the part of many Zen masters of anything that smacks of mere formalism. But it seems that most Japanese Zen masters simply followed Japanese (and Chinese) traditions and wrote farewell poems, although some of them suggest their objection to this custom in their own death poem.

DEATH POEMS: BETWEEN SOLEMNITY AND LAUGHTER

But for the deeply rooted conservatism of the Japanese people, their culture would not have preserved itself so well through so many centuries. Such conservatism, however, sometimes borders on blind worship of tradition and customs, with results that are often somewhat ridiculous. We have, for example, the ironic story of "a man who asked his poetry teacher to compose a death poem for his wife."[17] There is also the story of one Narushima Chuhachiro, a man who, "fearing that he might die without warning and be unable to write a farewell poem," began writing death poems at the age of fifty-odd years, sending them for criticism to his poetry master Reizei Tameyasu (eighteenth cent.). At the age of eighty, he wrote:

For eighty years and more,	*Yaso amari*
by the grace of my sovereign	*kimi to oya to no*
and my parents, I have lived	*megumi mote*
with a tranquil heart	*yo o tsuki hana ni*
between the flowers and the moon.	*yasuku sugitaru*

As usual, he sent the poem to Reizei, who replied in this wise: "When you reach age ninety, correct the first line."[18]

The hesitation between desire to write a death poem and aversion to an "unnatural" act is noticeable in the death poems of more than a few poets, as these examples from the present volume will show:

Whether or not a paradise	*Koshiraete*
awaits in the far reaches	*aru to mo shirazu*
of the west . . .	*nishi no oku*
	—SOA (1677–1742)

Death poems	*Jisei to wa*
are mere delusion—	*sunawachi mayoi*
death is death.	*tada shinan*
	—TOKO (1710–95)

Since I was born	*Umarete wa*
I have to die,	*shinuru hazu nari*
and so . . .	*sore naraba*
	—KISEI (1688–1764)

A warrior named Fuse Yajiro grew ill in the spring, and by autumn he was dying. He wrote this poem:

Before long	*Naki tama no*
I shall be a ghost	*kazu ni hairite*
but just now	*naku naka ni*
how they bite my flesh!	*uki akikaze no*
the winds of autumn.	*mi ni zo shiminuru*

After writing this poem so full of nostalgia for life, Fuse Yajiro recovered somewhat and lived on for another month. Something must have changed his mind about death, for in a mood of greater detachment, he wrote another death poem:

Seen from	*Kenkon no*
outside creation	*soto yori kore o*
earth and sky	*uchi mireba*
aren't worth	*hiuchibako ni mo*
a box of matches.	*taranu ametsuchi*[19]

However strange it may seem, many poets chose to end their lives with a satirical poem, and some even mock this mockery itself. One *kyoka* poet wrote down, before dying, the well-known death poem of another poet, prefacing it with the words "I borrowed this poem from someone," and adding after it, "This is the last act of plagiarism I shall commit in this world."[20]

Morikawa Kyoriku (1656–1715), a pupil of Basho's, also wrote a *kyoka* death poem. The poem and its background have been left for us:

> Kyoriku . . . came from an ancient samurai family and was a talented painter. When he became Basho's pupil, Basho said to him, "For painting, you shall be my master; for haiku, I shall be yours."
>
> Kyoriku was extremely proud of his talents and considered other poets no better than dogs. . . . He would boast of himself, "I alone have gone straight to the heart of Basho's poetry."
>
> Before his death, Kyoriku wrote:

Till now I thought	*Ima made wa*
that death befell	*heta ga shinu zo to*
the untalented alone.	*omoishi ni*
If those with talent, too, must die	*jōzu mo shineba*
surely they make a better manure?	*kuso jōzu kana*[21]

Another writer puts Kyoriku's apparent boastfulness in a

light that is probably more in keeping with the spirit of his death poem. When asked by a man to teach him the art of poetry, Kyoriku refused, saying that he was "not talented enough." Surprised at this answer, the man reminded Kyoriku of his extravagant praise of himself. To this Kyoriku answered, "All that is only a joke. Don't take it seriously."[22]

No less famous than Kyoriku is Yamazaki Sokan (died *c.* 1540), of samurai birth, a *renga* poet, and one of the first composers of haiku. The following death poem is attributed to him:

Should someone ask	*Sōkan wa*
where Sokan went,	*doko e to hito no*
just say,	*tōtareba*
"He had some business	*chito yōji ari*
in the other world."	*ano yo e to ie*

And an author named Hanabusa Ikkei (d. 1843) wrote:

I thought to live	*Ni- sambyaku*
two centuries, or three—	*ikiyō to koso*
yet here comes death	*omoishi ni*
to me, a child	*hachijūgo nite*
just eighty-five years old.	*fuji no wakajini*

A man named Kita Takekiyo (d. 1856) apparently prepared his own tombstone in the Nihon'enoki district of Edo. Two haiku poets—Takarai Kikaku (1661–1707) and Hanabusa Itcho (1652–1724)—had been laid to rest in an old temple there. Kita Takekiyo wrote before his death:

I come to my grave	*Kite mireba*
in Nihon'enoki	*Nihon'enoki mo*
and here, to my delight,	*omoshiroshi*
I find beside me Kikaku and Itcho	*hanashi no tomo wa*
friends I can talk to.	*Kikaku Itchō*

Conversing about poetry with Kikaku and Itcho is indeed a rosy picture of life beyond death.

Another poet who expected an entertaining afterlife was Moriya Sen'an (d. 1838):

Bury me when I die	*Ware shinaba*
beneath a wine barrel	*sakaya no kame no*
in a tavern.	*shita ni ikeyo*
With luck	*moshi ya shizuku no*
the cask will leak.	*moriyasennan*

The last line of the poem, "perhaps will leak," is similar to the pronunciation of the poet's name.

The merchants and artisans of the Edo period, like earlier monks and poets, spoke of this life in terms of a transient "floating world" *(ukiyo)*, or of a dream that vanishes, but rather than lift their eyes to the monasteries high in the mountains, they let their legs carry them to the geisha houses in the Yoshiwara quarter of Edo. "From all directions, the compass needle points to Yoshiwara," quips one *senryu* poet. In so hedonistic an atmosphere, a spirit of satire thrived, especially near the end of the period. Anything at all might fall victim to the *senryu* poets' sharp tongues, and it is no wonder that they do not spare the custom of writing death poems. How can a man know when he will die? And what happens to the poem should he get well again?

After recovery, he polishes the style of his death poem.	*Shinisokonōte jisei shinaosu*

The mouth that has uttered a death poem now devours porridge.	*Jisei no kuchi de kayu ni kuitsuku*

And when a man dies, so what if he has left a death poem?

The doctors praise his death poem and depart.	*Ishashū wa jisei o homete tatarekeri*

The poem pokes fun no less at the doctors than at the dying poet.

There were those among *senryu* poets who did not hesitate even to parody well-known death poems. Here is Basho's last poem:

On a journey, ill: my dream goes wandering over withered fields.	*Tabi ni yande yume wa kareno o kakemeguru*

A *senryu* poet writes:

Locked in my room: my dream goes wandering over brothels.	*Zashikirō yume wa kuruwa o kakemeguri*

The following *senryu* even takes an ironic view of another man's death scene:

The dying priest	*Nanimokamo*
looks as if	*satotta yō ni*
he knew it all.	*hotokemeki*

Though the next poem, too, looks humorously at death, there is a trace of pathos as well:

The last of human desire:	*Jin'yoku no*
he grasps at	*saigo kokū*
the air.	*tsukamu nari*

A death poem is liable to sound strained if its author racks his brain for an "appropriate" farewell, and not all death poems succeed in conveying the impact of this final experience. Sometimes, poems which are not specifically defined as "death poems" are more forceful. A well-known tanka poet, Shimaki Akahiko (1876–1926), wrote this poem not long before his death:

Where did that dog	*Waga ie no*
that used to be here go?	*inu wa izuko ni*
I thought about him	*yukinuramu*
once again tonight	*koyoi mo omoi*
before I went to bed.	*idete nemureru*

How is a person's poetry linked to his life? What can it tell of his death? One poet may search in vain for a poem as long as he lives; another repeats one poem again and again;

yet another lives and dies in every poem he creates. The experience of the renga poet Satomura Joha (1524–1602) was of the first type. Before his death, Joha said that if someone writing a poem prior to his at a *renga*-composition gathering had only suggested the phrase "a little of the sea" *(umi suko-shi),* he would have followed it with a phrase containing "Mount Osaka."* "I wished," he wrote, "for the phrase long ago, but no one ever started out like that, and now I must leave this life without having composed my verse."[23] Even if we were to analyze at length the images Joha wanted to combine, we would never understand the particular note he strove for all his life, a note only he could comprehend.

By contrast, Kashiku, a little-known poet from the late seventeenth or early eighteenth century, heard the same sound all his life, and this was the sound he repeated at his death:

> A certain man left his native province to wander from place to place. He was an artist and a haiku poet; he could dance, sing, and play stringed instruments; and he used to gladden the hearts of all who came near him. For a number of years he was part of the company around the table of Ozawa Sahichi, an innkeeper in the Tokaido region. One day Sahichi said to him, "I've been watching you for a long time. I can see that you're not a petty man: you're even-tempered, you avoid arguments, and you're free of vices. In fact, you've got all the makings of a monk. Why not shave your head and lead a monk's life, free of ties?" The man grew very happy when he heard this.

* Mount Osaka: in Shiga Prefecture, overlooking Lake Biwa. *Umi* and *osaka* also signify "birth" and "conjugal vows" respectively.

On the spot he shaved his hair, laughing, and said, "Ah! What a relief! I've been rid of 'the grease' [a metaphor— the expression refers to a plait of greased hair and here signifies relief from this life as well]." The innkeeper laughed with him and replied, "Since I'm the one who persuaded you, I'll give you the name you'll go by as a monk." He called him "Kashiku" [a formula similar to "yours sincerely," used by women at the close of letters]. Kashiku stayed on for several months more in Sahichi's inn, then decided to set out as a wandering monk. He went to Naniwa [Osaka], singing *kyoka* on his way, plucking stringed instruments, and begging rice from door to door. . . . Whenever he returned to Sahichi's inn, he need not have begged, as his many friends were willing to support him. But Kashiku, who hated flattery and false praise, refused all invitations to dine. When invited to a meal, he would answer, "I desire nothing but the view of Mount Fuji," and would turn his back and go. One day his corpse was found in the snow outside a temple gate. . . . He was dressed in beggar's clothing and wrapped in a straw gown. Beside his head lay a scrap of paper which read:

Mount Fuji's melting snow	*Fuji no yuki*
is the ink	*tokete suzuri no*
with which I sign	*sumigoromo*
my life's scroll,	*kashiku wa fude no*
"Yours sincerely."	*owari narikeri*[24]

The last poem left by Basho is generally considered his death poem, but Basho himself did not intend to write such a poem. When he was on his deathbed, his pupils hinted that he ought to leave one, but he replied that any of his poems could be his death poem. And indeed, in all of Basho's best poems, a resonance can be heard that seems to come from and return to the void.

A certain Japanese professor has defined Japanese culture as "a culture of death." In a long essay he argues that the "collective unconsciousness" of the Japanese is governed by a strong attraction toward death. His theory somehow explains even the peculiar five- and seven-beat rhythm that characterizes Japanese poetry. "If Freud was correct," his thesis concludes, "and the death wish is a basic desire in all human culture, then it can be admitted that one culture in particular may represent that desire."[25] Another professor claims, to the contrary, that the outstanding feature of Japanese culture is the love of the Japanese people for all phenomena. The Japanese, he says, are unwilling to believe in a reality separate from this world; they understand the abstract in terms of the world's concrete features—its mountains, rivers, trees, and insects.[26]

It is true that the millions of people living on the isles of Japan are a single nation, and a nation, so they say, has its own particular culture. Every student of that culture who explains it one way or another is probably correct from his point of view. Contradictory ideas may be found within a single person; how much more so, then, in an entire nation? Poems written before death no doubt reflect the attitudes of the dying, and what hundreds and thousands of Japanese say before death must certainly partake of the "Japanese spirit." Let us not forget, however, that when someone dies, it is not a nation but an individual that is dying. A person can bequeath his property and even his opinions to his survivors, but he buries his own name with him. And what stands behind that name, which belongs to the man alone, will never be understood by another. This is perhaps what a certain little-known poet named Tomoda Kimpei meant when he composed his death poem:

In life I never was	*Aru toki wa*
among the well-known flowers	*hana no kazu ni wa*
and yet, in withering	*taranu domo*
I am most certainly	*chiru ni wa morenu*
Tomoda Kimpei.	*Tomoda Kimpei*[27]

❖

NOTE ON THE POEMS

The names heading the poems in Part Two are generally the monastic names of the Zen monks; such a name is received when a monk enters an order. In Japan, well-known monks especially are known by their monastic names rather than their real ones. Written sources, however, may not always be consistent in listing a given person, sometimes using the real name, monastic name, pen name, and/or posthumous name. Where a single name appears in Part Three, it is the haiku poet's pen name, which is usually the name by which the poet is most well known. Occasionally, in cases in which a poet is a figure known in history and references by his real name, this name is given in the commentary. Where more than one name appears in the heading, these names are in most cases the poet's real name; apparently, these individuals did not use a pen name.

The poems in Parts Two and Three have been arranged in alphabetical order by the name of the poet for easy reference. Terms and concepts in the poems that require explanation are generally treated most fully the first time they appear. A full listing of such words is found in the Index of Poetic Terms (p. 349).

The traditional Japanese calendar, taken from the Chinese, is fundamentally a lunar one. The months have twenty-nine or thirty days, the first day of the month falling on the day of the new moon. A year consists of twelve months, 354 or 355 days; in order to adjust the calendar to the revolution of the earth around the sun, seven intercalary months are added in the course of nineteen-year cycles. The new year starts on the first new moon after the sun enters Aquarius, that is, between January 21 and February 19 (February 20 in the Orient).

In 1873 the Japanese adopted the Gregorian calendar used by the nations of the West. The months of death given in this book (when known) refer to those of the traditional calendar for poets who died before this change. For those who died in or after 1873, the date is given in terms of the Gregorian calendar, except when original sources give the date in terms of the old system.

In Japanese poetry, especially haiku, the use of images from nature and seasonal terms is very important. In death poems in particular, an image from the season in which the poet died is often included in the poem. Although the system was more complicated, the seasons correspond to the months in approximately the following manner: the first three months (about early February to early May) are spring; the fourth, fifth, and sixth months (early May to early August) are summer; the seventh, eighth, and ninth months (early August to early November) are autumn; and the last three months (early November to early February) are winter.

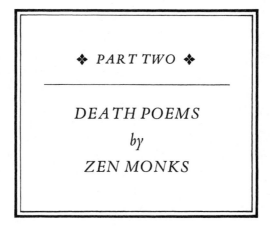

❖ *PART TWO* ❖

DEATH POEMS
by
ZEN MONKS

BASSUI TOKUSHO

抜 隊 得 勝

Died on the twentieth day of the second month, 1387
at the age of sixty-one

Look straight ahead. What's there?
If you see it as it is
You will never err.

When Bassui was about thirty-one years of age, he heard the running of water in a brook and was enlightened. Thereafter, he spent most of his days in a hut in the mountains. When people heard of the solitary monk and gathered to hear "the word," he would flee. In spite of his longing for solitude, Bassui did not turn his back on the simple people, but taught them Zen in words they could understand. He often warned his followers against the dangers of drinking, and forbade them to taste "even a single drop." On the margin of his portrait he wrote, "I teach with the voice of silence."

Just before his death Bassui turned to the crowd that had gathered around and said the words above. Repeating them in a loud voice, he died.

❖

DAIDO ICHI'I

大道一以

*Died on the twenty-sixth day of the second month, 1370
at the age of seventy-nine*

> A tune of non-being
> Filling the void:
> Spring sun
> Snow whiteness
> Bright clouds
> Clear wind.

❖

DAIGU SOCHIKU

大愚宗築

*Died on the sixteenth day of the seventh month, 1669
past the age of eighty*

Daigu was raised in a Zen monastery. While he was still a young monk, a woman asked him to hold a funeral service for her son. After the burial she asked, "Where has my child gone?" Daigu had no answer for her, and the incident shook him profoundly. He abandoned the monastery and went to be alone in the mountains.

Daigu was fond of drinking; it is said that he was usually half-drunk. He did not restrain his speech and used to insult people while conversing with them. In spite of his eccentricity, or perhaps because of it, people from all ranks of society were drawn to him, and they would come to him on the mountain to hear his words.

Daigu later moved to Edo, where he gave sanctuary in his temple to two women, mistresses of a daimyo from whom they had escaped. This act added to already existing rumors about Daigu's relationships with women, but Daigu gave them no heed. Because of the bad name such behavior gave him, his rise in the religious hierarchy was delayed, but Daigu himself did not care for power and authority. When an honorable post was at last offered him, he refused it on the grounds that he would be dismissed anyway because of his peculiar character.

The name Daigu, which the monk chose for himself, means "great fool." To his self-portrait he added these words: "This monk is bound in chains of ignorance and lust. He is not able to follow the way of the Buddha. As his name is, so is he—a great fool."

Lying on his deathbed, Daigu wrote the following:

> Needles pierce my ailing body, and my pain grows greater. This life of mine, which has been like a disease— what is its meaning? In all the world I haven't a single friend to whom I can unburden my soul. Truly all that appears to the eye is only a flower that blooms in a day.

Three days before his death Daigu wrote a short poem praising himself as "unique in his generation." At the end of the poem he put the words "three days before." Did he regret having boasted and wish to write a different poem? The following day he requested that his attendant bring him writing paper, and as the latter was about to hand it to his master, Daigu hit him. A day later Daigu died.

❖

DAIRIN SOTO

大林宗套

Died on the twenty-seventh day of the first month, 1568
at the age of eighty-nine

My whole life long I've sharpened my sword
And now, face to face with death
I unsheathe it, and lo—
The blade is broken—
Alas!

❖

DOKYO ETAN

道鏡慧端

Died on the sixth day of the tenth month, 1721
at the age of eighty

Here in the shadow of death it is hard
To utter the final word.
I'll only say, then,
"Without saying."

> Nothing more,
> Nothing more.

Dokyo, also known as Shoju Ronin, lived most of his life in a hut and refused to join the large monasteries. He saw in *zazen,* Zen meditation, the essence of the Zen way and used to deal harshly with believers who sought him out to hear so-called Zen doctrine. He would occasionally even draw his sword on them and drive them away, in keeping perhaps with his samurai origin. He is said to have once pushed the Zen master Hakuin from the pulpit when the latter rose to speak, whereupon Hakuin fainted from the force of the blow. For as long as Hakuin dwelt with him, Dokyo showed him no preference, and made him beg from door to door for his portion of rice like the other monks.

Dokyo wrote his last words while seated in the upright Zen position. Then he put down his brush, hummed "an ancient song" to himself, suddenly laughed out loud, and died.

❖

DOYU

道　祐

Died on the fifth day of the second month, 1256
at the age of fifty-six

> In all my six and fifty years
> No miracles occurred.

For the Buddhas and the Great Ones of the Faith,
I have questions in my heart.
And if I say,
"Today, this hour
I leave the world,"
There's nothing in it. Day after day,
Does not the sun rise in the east?

❖

ENNI BEN'EN

円爾弁円

*Died on the seventeenth day of the tenth month, 1280
at the age of seventy-nine*

All my life I taught Zen to the people—
Nine and seventy years.
He who sees not things as they are
Will never know Zen.

The sources say that Enni became ill at the beginning of the
summer. On the fifteenth day of the tenth month he an-
nounced to his followers that he was about to die. They did
not believe him. On the day of his death he ordered that the
drum be beaten and his imminent death proclaimed. He
sat down in his chair and wrote his last words. After adding
the date and his signature, he wrote "Farewell" and died.

Enni was also known as Shoichi Kasho and, after his death,
was called Shoichi Kokushi. Kokushi, "teacher of the nation,"

was a title given to a very revered priest. Enni was the first person to receive this title.

❖

GESSHU SOKO

月 舟 宗 胡

*Died on the tenth day of the first month, 1696
at the age of seventy-nine*

> Inhale, exhale
> Forward, back
> Living, dying:
> Arrows, let flown each to each
> Meet midway and slice
> The void in aimless flight—
> Thus I return to the source.

In the writings of the Taoist philosopher Lieh-tzu (fourth cent. B.C.), we find mention of two master archers whose arrows hit each other in midair. In the poem by Gesshu, the arrows do not fall back to the ground, but continue in a directionless flight through empty space. This image indicates a state of consciousness in which the concepts of the ordinary mind forming one's outlook on the world have vanished, and polarities (good–bad, life–death, etc.) are embraced in enlightened being.

❖

GIUN

義 雲

Died on the twelfth day of the tenth month, 1333
at the age of eighty-one

All doctrines split asunder
Zen teaching cast away—
Fourscore years and one.
The sky now cracks and falls
The earth cleaves open—
In the heart of the fire
Lies a hidden spring.

❖

GIZAN ZENRAI

儀 山 善 来

Died on the twenty-eighth day of March, 1878
at the age of seventy-seven

I was born into this world
I leave it at my death.
Into a thousand towns
My legs have carried me,
And countless homes—
What are all these?

> A moon reflected in the water
> A flower floating in the sky
> Ho!

"Ho!" is a translation of the word *totsu,* a kind of challenging cry uttered at the moment of enlightenment.

❖

GOKU KYONEN

悟 空 敬 念

Died on the eighth day of the tenth month, 1272
at the age of fifty-six

> The truth embodied in the Buddhas
> Of the future, present, past;
> The teaching we received from the
> Fathers of our faith
> Can all be found at the tip of my stick.

When Goku felt his death was near, he ordered all his monk-disciples to gather around him. He sat at the pulpit, raised his stick, gave the floor a single tap with it, and said the poem above. When he finished he raised the stick again, tapped the floor once more and cried, "See! See!" Then, sitting upright, he died.

❖

GUDO TOSHOKU

愚堂東寔

*Died on the first day of the tenth month, 1661
at the age of eighty-five*

Gudo was raised in a Zen monastery from the age of eight.
When he was nineteen, he left to wander up and down Japan
in search of the truth. Thus he later wrote, "I laugh at my-
self. After ten years of journeys and pilgrimages, here I am
knocking on the gates of Zen, my walking stick cracked
and my umbrella torn. The Buddha's teaching is basically
a simple matter: if you are hungry, eat rice; if you are thirsty,
drink tea; when it is cold, wrap yourself in a gown."

Gudo became a central figure in the Zen world of his time.
He was honored with the most illustrious title possible coming
from secular authorities—Kokushi, "teacher of the nation,"
a distinction generally reserved for the emperor's Zen teacher.
When past the age of eighty, he was still wandering through-
out Japan, seeing to the upkeep of temples and speaking to
believers.

It is said that at the age of eighty-two, Gudo was invited
by the emperor's father to speak before him. Midway through
his talk Gudo became sleepy; he stretched out on the floor
and began snoring loudly away. The father of the emperor
sat calmly by, looking at Gudo's aged face and waiting for
him to reawaken.

On the day of his death Gudo wrote, "I have finished my
task. It is now up to my followers to work for mankind."
He then put down his brush, yawned loudly, and died.

❖

HOSSHIN

法 心

Thirteenth century

> Coming, all is clear, no doubt about it.
> Going, all is clear, without a doubt.
> What, then, is it all?

Hosshin, also called Hosshimbo and Shosai, was a Japanese monk who sailed to China in the thirteenth century to study Zen. Since he could neither read nor write, his Chinese teacher drew a circle around the symbol 丁 and ordered the monk to meditate on that. Hosshin sat and reflected until "his rear became rotten and maggots bred there." This did not deter him from meditating, and he would see in everything the symbol. Only when the sign disappeared from his consciousness did he gain enlightenment.

A week before his death he declared, "I will die in seven days." No one heeded him, but on the seventh day following he spoke his last words as given above. When one of the monks requested that he add another phrase, Hosshin rebuked him with a sharp cry of *"Katsu!"* (a word signifying the attainment of enlightenment) and died.

❖

IKKYU SOJUN

一休宗純

*Died on the twenty-first day of the eleventh month, 1481
at the age of eighty-eight*

In all the kingdom southward
From the center of the earth
Where is he who understands my Zen?
Should the master Kido himself appear
He wouldn't be worth a worn-out cent.

Few children in Japan grow up ignorant of Ikkyu and the stories told about him. He was a monk, an author, and a poet, and his paintings, many of birds, are quite moving. Near the end of Ikkyu's life, the emperor put him in charge of Daitokuji in Kyoto, the chief temple of Rinzai Zen. More than either his literary and artistic talents or his religious message, however, his eccentric character was what made him the most famous of Japan's Zen masters. Ikkyu treated high and low, aristocrats and peasants, alike, and children loved him. He detested "intellectual Zen," and it is said that he once burned all the manuscripts in his possession. He avoided neither taverns nor brothels, and he never held his tongue.

The kingdom described in Ikkyu's poem is the continent southward from Mount Shumi (Skt., Sumeru), a mythical peak which, according to ancient Indian tradition, stands at the center of the world. The four kingdoms extending from the mountain's four sides are supposed to contain all of humanity. The southern continent includes India, China, and

Japan, the countries where Buddha's doctrine had been spread. The question "Where is he who understands my Zen?" is not to be taken as a boast. Where Zen ceases to be a doctrine and becomes reality, each individual stands alone, and no one can take his place. This being so, even the Chinese Zen master Kido Chigu (Hsü-tang Chih-yü, 1185–1269), whom Ikkyu considered his spiritual father, could neither add to nor detract from what Ikkyu was at that moment—an old man of eighty-eight years about to die.

Many of Ikkyu's writings deal with death. One of them ends with the following words: "And now, at the hour of my death, my bowels move—an offering raised to the Lord of Worlds." The frankness of the statement is characteristic of his style, but it ought not to be taken as profane. The image of a dying man who can no longer control his body and who defecates in his bed is no less "sacred" than that of a believer who brings flowers as an offering to his god; all is accepted with equanimity by the Lord of Worlds, the god Bonten (Skt., Brahmadeva).

❖

INGO

院 豪

*Died on the twenty-first day of the eighth month, 1281
at the age of seventy-two*

Three and seventy years
I've drawn pure water from the fire—

Now I become a tiny bug.
With a touch of my body
I shatter all worlds.

❖

KAISEN SHOKI

快 川 紹 喜

Died on the third day of the fourth month, 1582

In 1582 the samurai leader Oda Nobunaga (1534–82) captured a company of over one hundred Buddhist monks who were allies of his enemy. He ordered his men to pile dry branches around the prisoners and set fire to them all. Among the monks thus burned alive was Kaisen Shoki. According to one of the versions relating the last moments of this Zen master, one of his students asked him, "We cannot escape the passing away of all things in this world. Where now shall we turn in our search for the everlasting?" Kaisen replied, "Here it is before your eyes, in this very place." The monk pressed further, "What place is this before my eyes?" With flames licking upward at his body, Kaisen responded, "If you have vanquished your selfhood, coolness will rise even from the fire."

❖

KASO SODON

華叟宗曇

*Died on the twenty-seventh day of the sixth month, 1428
at the age of seventy-seven*

> A drop of water freezes instantly—
> My seven years and seventy.
> All changes at a blow
> Springs of water welling from the fire.

Kaso was the teacher of Ikkyu (p. 102) and Yoso (p. 127).
His comparison of his seventy-seven-year-long life to "a drop
of water [that] freezes instantly" symbolizes transience, the
essence of this world of senses according to Buddhist doc-
trine. The "blow" that changes all refers to enlightenment: a
thing no longer contradicts its opposite, and time and space
are no longer perceived through the concepts of the ordinary
mind. Life may seem to flee in a moment, but when the mind
is freed of the veil of ignorance and illusion that comes be-
tween the mind and the truth, life and death are only oppo-
site sides of the same coin—"water welling from the fire."

❖

KOGAKU SOKO

古岳宗亘

*Died on the twenty-fourth day of the sixth month, 1548
at the age of eighty-four*

My final words are these:
As I fall I throw all on a high mountain peak—
Lo! All creation shatters; thus it is
That I destroy Zen doctrine.

❖

KOGETSU SOGAN

江月宗玩

Died on the first day of the tenth month, 1643
at the age of seventy

Katsu!
Katsu!
Katsu!
Katsu!

The word *katsu* cannot really be translated conceptually. It is a sharp cry used by the Zen teacher and pupil at the moment of enlightenment. The cry appears in many Chinese and Japanese Zen writings and can be heard even today within monastery walls.

❖

KOHO KENNICHI

高 峰 顕 日

Died on the twentieth day of the tenth month, 1316
at the age of seventy-six

To depart while seated or standing is all one.
All I shall leave behind me
Is a heap of bones.
In empty space I twist and soar
And come down with the roar of thunder
To the sea.

Death in a Zen sitting position or death standing up was considered worthy of an enlightened person.

❖

KOKEI SOCHIN

古 渓 宗 陳

Died on the seventeenth day of the first month, 1597
at the age of sixty-six

For over sixty years
I often cried *Katsu!* to no avail.
And now, while dying,
Once more to cry *Katsu!*
Won't change a thing.

On the second day of the eighth month, 1596, the sixty-five-year-old Kokei took ill. Certain he would die soon, he composed his death poem. When he had finished reciting it, he "died." After six hours, however, he revived and began preaching to the monks who had gathered around his bed. Kokei abandoned the world for good about five months later.

❖

KOZAN ICHIKYO

固山一鞏

Died on the twelfth day of the second month, 1360
at the age of seventy-seven

> Empty-handed I entered the world
> Barefoot I leave it.
> My coming, my going—
> Two simple happenings
> That got entangled.

A few days before his death, Kozan called his pupils together, ordered them to bury him without ceremony, and forbade them to hold services in his memory. He wrote this poem on the morning of his death, laid down his brush, and died sitting upright.

❖

MUMON GENSEN

無 文 元 選

Died on the twenty-second day of the third month, 1390
at the age of sixty-eight

Life is an ever-rolling wheel
And every day is the right one.
He who recites poems at his death
Adds frost to snow.

*   *   *   *

Life is like a cloud of mist
Emerging from a mountain cave
And death
A floating moon
In its celestial course.
If you think too much.
About the meaning they may have
You'll be bound forever
Like an ass to a stake.

These are two separate poems. They were spoken, apparently
one after the other, just before Mumon's death.

❖

MUSHO JOSHO

無象静照

Died on the fifteenth day of the fifth month, 1306
at the age of seventy-three

When it comes—just so!
When it goes—just so!
Both coming and going occur each day.
The words I am speaking now—just so!

The sources tell us that on the day of his death, Musho sum-
moned the other monks, arranged for his burial service, said
his last words, and died sitting upright.

"Just so!" or "Thus!" *(nyoze)* is a cry used by the Zen
master to direct his pupil's attention to "things as they are"
or to indicate that the student sees things clearly.

❖

MUSO SOSEKI

夢窓疎石

Died on the thirtieth day of the ninth month, 1351
at the age of seventy-seven

Thus have I rolled my life throughout
Inside and out, reclined, upright.
What is all this?

A beating drum
A trumpet's blare
No more.

❖

NAMPO JOMYO

南 浦 紹 明

*Died on the twenty-ninth day of the twelfth month, 1308
at the age of seventy-four*

In 1307, exactly a year before his death, Nampo wrote:

This year, the twenty-ninth of the twelfth
No longer has a place to come to.
The twenty-ninth of the twelfth next year
Already has no place to go.

These words were taken, after his death, as proof that Nampo
knew he would die in a year. And so it was: on the twenty-
ninth day of the twelfth month, 1308, Nampo took up his
brush, wrote the following poem, and died.

To hell with the wind!
Confound the rain!
I recognize no Buddha.
A blow like the stroke of lightning—
A world turns on its hinge.

❖

RANKEI DORYU

蘭 渓 道 隆

Died in 1278
at the age of sixty-six

Thirty years and more
I worked to nullify myself.
Now I leap the leap of death.
The ground churns up
The skies spin round.

❖

SEIGAN SOI

清 岩 宗 渭

Died on the twenty-first day of the eleventh month, 1661
at the age of seventy-four

Joy of living,
Living joy. . . .
Zen doctrine is null.
Before I die,
Here is the secret of my teaching—
My staff nods in agreement.
            Katsu!

To these words Seigan added the date of his death, pressed his seal, and ended with "Farewell."

❖

SEISETSU SHUCHO

誠 拙 周 樗

Died on the twenty-eighth day of the sixth month, 1820
at the age of seventy-six

> My hour draws near and I am still alive.
> Drawn by the chains of death
> I take my leave.
> The King of Hades has decreed
> Tomorrow I shall be his slave.

According to ancient tradition in India, "the King of Hades," Emma-o (Skt., Yamaraja), is the underground ruler of the dead.

❖

SENGAI GIBON

仙 厓 義 梵

Died on the seventh day of the tenth month, 1837
at the age of eighty-eight

> He who comes knows only his coming
> He who goes knows only his end.
> To be saved from the chasm
> Why cling to the cliff?
> Clouds floating low
> Never know where the breezes will blow them.

Sengai is one of the most colorful figures in Japanese history—a Zen monk, a painter, and a poet. His drawings and writings, both done with a flourish, vibrate with Zen insight and humor.

Sengai gives one to understand, in many of his poems and sketches, that a "lifeless" life is not worth living. He once presented to a newlywed a marriage present, a *senryu* written in her honor and urging her thus:

> Young bride
> Be alive till they say to you
> Die! Die!

In one of his sketches, a bent and bald old man is trying to outwit death. Above the picture Sengai wrote:

> If you say, "Come back later,"
> He will speedily come to snatch you away.
> Say rather, "I shall not be in till I'm ninety-nine."

❖

SHUMPO SOKI

春浦宗熙

Died on the fourteenth day of the first month, 1496
at the age of eighty-eight

> My sword leans against the sky.
> With its polished blade I'll behead
> The Buddha and all of his saints.
> Let the lightning strike where it will.

It is said that after reciting this poem, Shumpo gave a single "laugh of derision" and died. To "behead / The Buddha" suggests spiritual independence and an awareness freed from the manner of thought dictated by religious tradition. According to Buddhist belief, a man who sins against religion and morality is liable to die by a stroke of lightning.

Several years before his death, as the disease which caused it worsened, Shumpo took leave of his disciples and followers with the following words:

> At times I supported the sky, at times the earth; at times I turned into a dragon, at times to a snake. I wandered at will through the cycles of life and of death. All the fathers of our faith I took into my mouth. I give as I will and I take as I will. I slash the leopard with my teeth; my spirit smashes mountains.

After saying these words he let out a sharp cry of *"Katsu!"*

Shumpo directed his disciples to burn his corpse and bury the ashes in the ground, forbidding them to erect a burial stone in his memory. He ended his will with the following poem:

> No single bone in my body is holy—
> It is but an ash heap of stinking bones.
> Dig a deep hole and there bury these remains
> Thus, not a grain of dust will stain
> The green mountains.

❖

SHUN'OKU SOEN

春屋宗園

Died on the ninth day of the second month, 1611
at the age of eighty-three

> Adrift between the earth and sky
> I call to the east and change it to west.
> I flourish my staff and return once again
> To my source.
> *Katsu!*

It is written that on the day of his death Shun'oku sensed that his end was near. He requested his attendant to hold his brush and dictated his death poem to him. Then he himself took the brush, wrote the date, signed his name and wrote "Farewell." He breathed his last a short while afterward.

❖

SUZUKI SHOSAN

鈴木正三

*Died on the twenty-fifth day of the sixth month, 1655
at the age of seventy-seven*

Shosan was born into a samurai family, and he fought in his master's service until his forty-second year. While still a warrior, he visited Zen masters to ask about "the matter of life and death." In 1620 he abandoned the way of the warrior and became a monk. He hated sectarianism and felt repulsed by an institutional framework. He thus never joined any one monastery, but chose instead to wander from one monastery to another, speaking to people and writing on Buddhist doctrine in a simple style that was understood by all. He often criticized organized religion and warned believers against the pursuit of honor and riches. Buddhism, he wrote, is not an abstract doctrine, but a way of life: for the warrior, the warrior's way; for the peasant, the peasant's way; for the artisan, the artisan's way; and for the merchant, the merchant's way. A person may choose whatever sect and manner of praying that suits him, provided he stays in the way with all his heart. As befit a man of samurai status, Shosan emphasized that the most important thing is to "look straight at death. To know death—that is the entire doctrine."

In the spring of 1655 Shosan became ill. When told that his illness was a grave one, he stated that it meant nothing, since he had already died more than thirty years before (when he became a monk?). As his condition became critical his followers gathered around his deathbed. One of them asked him to say "his final words." Shosan looked sharply at the monk and scolded him: "What are you saying? You only show that you don't understand what I've been saying for more than thirty years. Like this, I simply die."

❖

TAIGEN SOFU

太 原 崇 孚

Died on the tenth day of the intercalary month, 1555
at the age of sixty

I raise the mirror of my life
Up to my face: sixty years.
With a swing I smash the reflection—
The world as usual
All in its place.

❖

TAKUAN SOHO

沢 庵 宗 彭

Died on the eleventh day of the twelfth month, 1645
at the age of seventy-three

Takuan's personality was extraordinary. He was a scholar, a painter, and a poet, close to the court, and admired by rulers and common people alike, although he refused to regard anyone as his disciple, for he did not consider himself a teacher. At the age of thirty-seven he was appointed head monk of Daitokuji temple in Kyoto. Takuan, who hated having power and authority, abandoned the temple after three days. He turned down honorary titles, and when he was invited by the shogun to serve under him, he refused. He once disobeyed the shogun and was exiled to the distant hills. When his banishment was lifted and he was ordered to return to the city, Takuan replied that he preferred the mountains and had no desire to return to the "filthy and crowded" Edo.

Lying on his deathbed, Takuan at first refused to write a death poem. At last he gave in to the entreaties of those surrounding him, took up his brush, and drew the character for "dream," shown above. When he finished, he threw the brush down and died. Takuan had requested beforehand that his body be burned on a mountain, that no burial service be held, and that no tombstone be put up for him.

❖

TETSUGEN DOKO

鉄 眼 道 光

*Died on the twenty-second day of the third month, 1682
at the age of fifty-three*

Full of great changes
My three and fifty years have been.
I commented on the holy writ—a heavy sin
That echoes to the skies.
Now I will sail on the lake of lotus blooms
And break into the skies within the water.

Tetsugen is known as a scholar who edited, wrote commentaries on, and published many Zen writings. Such an undertaking might be considered praiseworthy in some religions, but many Zen Buddhists believe that Zen must be taught "not by means of the written word, but by a pointed finger." Tetsugen did not, however, let words stand between him and life.

In 1682 there was a famine in Japan. Tetsugen used his entire fortune, which had been dedicated to the printing of Buddhist texts, to distribute food to the hungry. "To feed the poor we must sell the temples and holy writings," he said. It is said that in giving aid to the starving he knew no fatigue, and that through contact with them "fleas stuck to his gown." His efforts saved about ten thousand people.

In the same year, Tetsugen's strength gave out, and he became ill and died. His funeral was attended by approximately one hundred thousand people, many of whom he had saved from famine, and "the sound of the mourners' weeping shook the fields and the forests."

Buddhist tradition envisions paradise as a lake covered with lotus plants.

❖

TETTO GIKO

徹 翁 義 亨

Died on the fifteenth day of the fifth month, 1369
at the age of seventy-five

I look now at the very moment
Even the Buddha is dumbfounded.
All turns with a swing.
I land on the plain of nothingness.

Tetto wrote his death poem on the last day of his life. Several days before his death, he had given a sealed message to his followers, forbidding them to read it while he was alive. After he died they read the following words:

The truth is never taken
From another.
One carries it always
By oneself.
Katsu!

❖

TOSUI UNKEI

桃水雲渓

Died on the nineteenth day of the ninth month, 1683
past the age of seventy

Seventy years and more
I have tasted life to its utmost.
The stench of urine sticks to my bones.
What matter all these?
Ho! Where is the place I return to?
Above the peak the moonlight whitens
A clear wind blows.

Tosui, who was called by all "the holy beggar," entered a
monastery at the age of seven. As an adolescent he often
fasted and secluded himself. He refused to join any one sect
and never stayed long in one place. In one of the monasteries
where he spent several years, he found himself—against his
will—teaching Zen. At the height of the teaching season he
wrote the following words on the monastery gate before
abandoning the place:

Today is the end of religion's work—
Go back, all of you, to your homes.
I leave before you,
Eastward or westward,
Wherever the wind might carry me.

After wandering throughout Japan, Tosui joined the
beggars of Kyoto and lived among them. One day one of

his former pupils found him there. Tosui was dressed in rags, his hair growing wildly, and he carried a straw mat on his back. The pupil asked to join him, but Tosui rebuked him and tried to send him away. In spite of this the young monk put on begging clothes and followed his master. Tosui spoke not a word to him. In the town of Katata near Lake Biwa the two of them found the corpse of a beggar and buried it. When the pupil exclaimed, "Poor man," Tosui turned to him and scolded him: "Why pity the man? The most honored of men and the most wretched of beggars share a single fate—death." Tosui then sat to eat the rice porridge that the beggar had left, murmuring as he ate it, "Mm, good." Suddenly he turned to his pupil and ordered him, "Eat this!" As he had no choice but to obey, the pupil placed a small portion of the porridge in his mouth, but he was unable to swallow it and gagged it up again. "I warned you not to follow me," Tosui reproached him, and sent him away.

Thus it was that Tosui wandered from place to place, supporting himself by weaving straw boots to cover the legs of horses in winter and by carrying people on his back. For a while he lived in the city of Otsu (Shiga Prefecture) under a straw roof stretched over the space between two storehouses. At the same time, a certain stable hand, who considered Tosui a holy man, brought him a portrait of the Buddha Amida. On the picture Tosui wrote the following verse:

> Though my dwelling be small
> I take you in, Lord Amida—
> But don't think for a minute
> I need you for life after death.

Tosui spent the last years of his life in Kyoto, living at first under a bridge and later in a half-demolished shack in the outskirts of the city. He died sitting upright in a Zen position, his death poem lying beside his body.

❖

TOYO EICHO

東 陽 英 朝

Died on the twenty-fourth day of the eighth month, 1504
at the age of seventy-seven

> All four pillars of enlightenment
> Crumble at once—
> See! See!
> Moonlight wreathing coral branches—
> What does it mean?
> Now all grows as dark
> As the palace of hell in
> The grasp of Satan
> > *Katsu!*

Toyo wrote these words while sitting upright; he then put down his brush and died.

The "four pillars of enlightenment" are four qualities ascribed to nirvana by Buddhist scriptures: everlastingness, contentment, truth (liberation from the illusions of self), and purity. Nirvana is described as a state beyond life and death, but while dying Toyo looks straight at death and sees in it the naked truth of absolute destruction. For a moment he considers the image of perfection and harmony (the moon lighting the corals in the water), but this vision gives way to a darker one of death. The final *"Katsu!"* wipes out the several images and brings the poem back to the here and now at the moment of death.

❖

TSUGEN JAKUREI

通 幻 寂 霊

Died on the fifth day of the fifth month, 1391
at the age of seventy

From the day of my coming hither
Full seventy years have passed.
Now, setting out on my final path
My two legs trample the sky.

❖

UNGO KIYO

雲 居 希 膺

Died on the eighth day of the eighth month, 1659
at the age of seventy-seven

> I came into the world after Buddha.
> I leave the world before Miroku.
> Between the Buddha of the beginning
>   and the Buddha of the end
> I am not born, I do not die.

On the first day of the eighth month, 1659, Ungo shut himself up in his room and prepared for the end. On the eighth day he emerged and gave a sealed envelope to the monk who attended him. He then called his pupils together and preached to them one final time. In the middle of his sermon, exactly at noon, he died. When his pupils opened the envelope they found his last words.

The historical Buddha is Gautama Siddhartha (sixth to fifth cents. B.C.), also called Shakyamuni, "the sage from the Shakya clan," the founder of Buddhism. Miroku (Skt., Maitreya) is the name of a mythical Buddha who is seated in the heavens and who will in the last days (5 billion 670 million years after Shakyamuni's death) inherit the place now occupied by the historical Buddha. These two personages mark the beginning and end of historical time. Ungo does not deny his own existence in time as a person who was born, who lived in a certain period, and who died. By "I am not born, I do not die," he indicates the level at which his consciousness dwells. On this level, life and death are nothing but illusions of the imagination.

❖

YAKUO TOKUKEN

約翁德儉

Died on the nineteenth day of the fifth month, 1320
at the age of seventy-six

My six and seventy years are through.
I was not born, I am not dead.
Clouds floating on the high wide skies
The moon curves through its million-mile course.

Two days before his death, Yakuo called his fellow monks together and said, "The words of a man before he dies are no small matter. This is a barrier that all must pass through. Tell me each of you what you think about that." The monks answered in various ways, and Yakuo neither approved nor disapproved. The next day he ordered his pupils to burn his body and forbade them to hold an elaborate burial ceremony. "Tomorrow morning," he said, "I shall eat the rice porridge with you for breakfast, and at noon I shall go." The following day at noon he wrote his final words, threw the brush from his hand, and died sitting upright.

❖

YOSO SOI

養叟宗頤

Died on the twenty-seventh day of the sixth month, 1458
at the age of eighty-three

> *Katsu!*
> On the death bed—*Katsu!*
> Let he who has eyes see!
> *Katsu! Katsu! Katsu!*
> And once again, *Katsu!*
> *Katsu!*

Yoso was a pupil of Kaso's (p. 105). When Kaso died, Yoso, then fifty-three years old, pledged to himself that he would leave the world on the same day of the same month as his master. And so it was that thirty years to the day after Kaso's death, this vow was fulfilled.

Yoso asked his attendant to hold his brush and to write his death poem during his very last moments. Whatever the meaning hidden in Yoso's "*Katsu!*" may be, there is certainly an appeal to look straight at an eighty-three-year-old man about to die.

❖

ZOSAN JUNKU

蔵 山 順 空

Died on the fifth day of the fifth month, 1308
at the age of seventy-six

> You must play
> The tune of non-being yourself—
> Nine summits collapse
> Eight oceans go dry.

The "tune of non-being" does not refer to death, but to a state wherein the enlightened awareness is no longer bound by such polarities as life and death. "Nine summits" separated by "eight oceans" represent the world as pictured in Indian myth. The tallest mountain, Mount Shumi, stands in the center, surrounded by the eight other peaks. Death is here described as a cosmic event, together with the consciousness that the world and all within it disappears.

❖

ZOSO ROYO

蔵叟朗誉

Died on the fifth day of the sixth month, 1276
at the age of eighty-four

I pondered Buddha's teaching
A full four and eighty years.
The gates are all now locked about me.
No one was ever here—
Who then is he about to die,
And why lament for nothing?
Farewell!
The night is clear,
The moon shines calmly,
The wind in the pines
Is like a lyre's song.
With no I and no other
Who hears the sound?

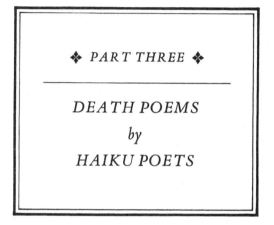

❖ *PART THREE* ❖

DEATH POEMS
by
HAIKU POETS

AKI-NO-BO

秋 之 坊

Died on the fourth day of the first month, 1718

The fourth day	*Shōgatsu yokka*
of the new year: what better day	*yorozu kono yo o*
to leave the world?	*saru ni yoshi*

In the traditional Japanese calendar, there are "good days" and "bad days." The custom, which is followed to a certain extent even today, is to have ceremonies and other events take place on days of good fortune, and to avoid performing important activities on days of bad fortune. The first three days of the new year are good days. New Year's celebrations cease by the fourth day, and with them ends good fortune.

One account of Aki-no-Bo's death is as follows:

Aki-no-Bo died on the fourth day of the first month. On the very day he was visited by his friend, the poet Rito. As was his custom, Aki-no-Bo stretched out on his stomach and chatted with Rito. Among other things, he said, "I made a calendar [a collection of poems, one for each day of the year]. Listen to this: 'The fourth day / of the new year: what better day / to leave the world?'" Aki-no-Bo had no sooner finished reciting the verse than he nodded his head and died. Filled with wonder, Rito thought about how Aki-no-Bo had always lived

133

forgetful of himself, now dying in the same way. With tears of sorrow and admiration streaming from his eyes, Rito composed on the spot the following poem: "He made as if to be asleep / and slipped away / Aki-no-Bo [*Inetsumu to / misete usekeri / Aki-no-Bo*]." Rito buried his friend, who had lived as a monk with no family, with due pomp and ceremony.[1]

The authenticity of this version has been doubted, because the death poem above appears seven years before Aki-no-Bo's death, written by the poet Ryoto (p. 269). However, as the source of the story is generally quite trustworthy, it can be granted that the poet died as described, and that he merely borrowed his last poem from his contemporary Ryoto.

It is known that Aki-no-Bo was of the samurai class and that he became a monk. He lived in a hut which he built on temple grounds in the city of Kanazawa. His shack was called Shujitsu-an, "hut of the autumn sun." (The name Aki-no-Bo means "autumn monk.") He lived a life of poverty and on winter days would borrow charcoal to keep himself warm.

Aki-no-Bo met the poet Basho twice, once in 1689 and once in 1690. At their first meeting the two of them are said to have sat together without exchanging a single word. The second time, Basho dedicated a poem to the monk:

No sign
in the cicada's song
that it will soon be gone

*Yagate shinu
keshiki wa miezu
semi no koe*

❖

AMANO HACHIRO

天 野 八 郎

*Died on the fifth day of the eleventh month, 1868
at the age of thirty-eight*

Lightning flickers	*Kita ni nomi*
only in the north:	*inazuma arite*
the moon is overcast.	*tsuki kurashi*

In 1868 a new political and social order began in Japan with the Meiji Restoration. The armies of several fiefs *(han)* rebelled against the Tokugawa shogun, forced him to surrender, and took over Edo, the capital. This put an end to the long rule of the Tokugawa, and governmental authority was restored, in appearance at least, to the emperor. The greater part of the army of the shogunate surrendered, but its fleet retreated to the island of Hokkaido and continued in its resistance to the new rule until May 1869. Hachiro, who supported the old regime, tried to join the shogun's forces in Hokkaido, but he was captured and thrown into prison, where he died.

The reference to lightning in the north is not only a summer image, but an allusion to the last bulwark of the old regime's supporters in the north of Japan.

❖

ARIMARU

蟻 丸

Died in the twelfth month, 1703

Running shallow   *Kawa no se ni*
with a year's end sound: *shiwasu no oto no*
river rapids.   *nagarekeri*

❖

ASEI

蛙 井

Died in 1752

Flowers of the grass: *Nora ni saku*
scarcely shown, and withered   *na wa kore made zo*
name and all.   *kusa no hana*

The blossoming of cherries in the spring evokes in haiku
poets a feeling of wonder at nature's beauty. But facing the
blossoming of grasses and nameless field and garden flowers
at the beginning of autumn, Asei grieves for that which comes
and goes, yet leaves no lasting impression.

❖

ATSUJIN

日 人

Died on the thirtieth day of the fourth month, 1836
at the age of seventy-nine

Earth and metal . . .	*Tsuchi kane ya*
although my breathing ceases	*iki wa taete mo*
time and tide go on.	*tsukihi ari*

Tsuchi means "earth" and *kane* is "metal." There is no particular significance in the combination *tsuchi kane,* and the poet's intention is not clear.

❖

BAIKA

梅 價

Died on the third day of the third month, 1843
at the age of seventy

People, when you see the smoke,	*No o yaku to*
do not think	*hito na omoi so*
it is fields they're burning.	*hito-kemuri*

On clear days without wind at the beginning of spring, village people gather to burn off the withered fields of winter.

The burning fertilizes the ground and rids it of harmful insects. Here, however, the poet refers to the smoke rising from the cremation of his body.

❖

BAIKO

梅 幸

Died in February, 1903
at the age of sixty

Plum petals falling	*Chiru ume ni*
I look up—the sky,	*miaguru sora no*
a clear crisp moon.	*tsuki kiyoshi*

The *ume* is a variety of plum found in the Far East. This tree holds an important place in the literature of China and Japan. In ancient Japanese literature the word *hana,* "flower," meant "plum blossom," and only later did the cherry replace the plum as the symbol for blooming in general. Ancient tradition even treats the plum as a holy tree. The plum blossoms earlier than other trees, sometimes at the end of winter or the first of spring, even before it has budded leaves. The commonest variety has white flowers which give off a strong scent.

❖

BAINEN

梅　年

Died on the twelfth day of January, 1905
at the age of eighty

Now spring has come
into my world:
farewell!

Itomagoi
wagayo-no-haru no
kitarikeri

❖

BAIRYU

梅　笠

Died on the eleventh day of the sixth month, 1863
at the age of fifty-nine

O hydrangea—
you change and change
back to your primal color.

Ajisai ya
kawari kawarite
moto no iro

The hydrangea *(ajisai)* is a bush from one to two meters high. Its thick leaves are saw-toothed and armed with sharp edges. In the summer its flowers bloom in clusters. The common name for the flower is *nanabake,* "seven changes," as it changes color seven times, from shades of green to yellow, blue, purple, pink, and finally back to green. This flower was introduced to the West by the German doctor Philipp Franz van Siebold (1796–1866), one of the first Western men to teach the Japanese medicine, languages, and sciences, and one of the first to investigate the history, geography, and folklore of Japan.

❖

BAISEI

梅 星

Died on the first day of the first month, 1745

Island of Eternity:	*Hōrai ya*
a turtle dries its shell out	*kame mo kō hosu*
in the first sun rays of the year.	*hatsu-hinata*

The word *horai* initially meant one of the three mountains in "the islands of paradise," where, according to a Chinese fable, the secret of immortality is found. In Japan the word came to be used for various New Year's foods and decorations, all of which are associated, in one way or another, with longevity. The turtle *(kame),* itself a symbol of long life, is pictured in Chinese and Japanese paintings as floating on the surface of water and carrying Mount Horai on its back. For this reason, the turtle appears among New Year's decorations in Japan.

The first rays of the sun on New Year's Day are called *hatsu-hi;* many Japanese stay up all night to be sure to see these. *Hatsu-hinata,* "first sun-basking," seems to be a word made up by Baisei. Did he watch the sun lighting up the turtle decoration in his house, or did he see a vision of that mythical turtle floating on the sunlit ocean, carrying on its back the "Island of Eternity"?

❖

BAISEKI

梅　石

Died on the sixteenth day of the ninth month, 1716
at the age of sixty-seven

The journey west,	*Daremo negau*
a way that all would travel:	*hanano o nishi e*
flower field.	*angya kana*

In the Jodo, or Pure Land, sects of Buddhism, it is believed that the dead are born anew in the Pure Land in the West ruled by Amida, the Buddha of Everlasting Light. Death is often pictured as a journey westward.

❖

BAKO

馬　光

Died on the first day of the fifth month, 1751
at the age of sixty-five

Looking back at the valley: *Furikaeru*
no more dwellings, only   *tani no to mo nashi*
the cuckoo cries.   *hototogisu*

The *hototogisu,* a species of cuckoo, winters in southern Asia and migrates to Japan in the middle of May, where it stays until autumn, its voice echoing across the plains and hills. The female lays her eggs in the nest of the nightingale, shoving the nightingale eggs out of the nest to make room for her own. One written form of *hototogisu* consists of the Chinese characters for "time" and "bird." This "bird of time" often appears in poetry as a messenger of death.

❖

BANKOKU

盤 谷

*Died on the third day of the eleventh month, 1748
at the age of seventy*

The longest winter night: *Tōji ume*
plum petals fall and finally   *chiri yuku hate ga*
the western moon.   *nishi no tsuki*

Toji, the winter solstice, is the shortest day of the year, falling north of the equator on December twenty-first or twenty-second. The "western moon" *(nishi no tsuki)* alludes to the Pure Land in the West.

❖

BANZAN

晚　山

*Died on the fifteenth day of the eighth month, 1730
at the age of sixty-nine*

Farewell—
I pass as all things do
dew on the grass.

*Mame de iyo
mi wa narawashi no
kusa no tsuyu*

Dew *(tsuyu),* covering the grass and trees of autumn, evaporates as the sun rises. Dew is one of the images signifying transience in Japanese poetry, and Buddhist literature often refers to the world as "a world of dew."

❖

BASHO

芭　蕉

*Died on the twelfth day of the tenth month, 1694
at the age of fifty-one*

On a journey, ill:
my dream goes wandering
over withered fields.

*Tabi ni yande
yume wa kareno o
kakemeguru*

This is the last poem of one of the greatest haiku poets. Basho had fallen seriously ill on one of his travels. When his pupils hinted that he ought to leave a farewell poem, he replied that any of his poems could be his death poem. Nevertheless, on the eighth day of the tenth month, after gathering his pupils around his bed, he wrote this poem. He died four days later.

❖

BENSEKI

鞭 石

*Died on the fifteenth day of the second month, 1728
at the age of eighty*

Child of the way,	*Tsui ni yuku*
I leave at last—	*kishi no yanagi ya*
a willow on the other shore.	*nori no chigo*

Nori no chigo, "child of the way," expresses not only the dream of an eighty-year-old man to renew his youth, but contains a play on words as well. In his last years Benseki abandoned the world and became a monk, changing his name to Honi, the Chinese-derived pronunciation of the characters used to write *nori no [chi]go*. "Honi" can mean both "child of the way" and "child of the doctrine."

The willow *(yanagi)*, common throughout Japan, is a tall tree that grows on the banks of rivers and lakes, its slender branches stretching down as thin as strings. A willow tree is often mentioned in haiku as a picture of spring, its branches covered with green and drifting in the wind.

The image of a journey from one bank of a river to the other appears often in Buddhist literature as a symbol of the transition from the state of ignorance and illusion to that of enlightenment.

❖

BOKUKEI

木 鶏

Died on the sixteenth day of the fifth month, 1869

Cuckoo, I too	*Hototogisu*
sing, spitting blood	*ware mo chi o haku*
my welling thoughts . . .	*omoi kana*

Bokukei (Nakajima Saburosuke) fell in battle against the emperor's army in the Meiji Restoration. He was a friend of Hogyoku's (p. 188) and died five days after him, together with his own two sons.

The cuckoo has a red mouth, and because of this, or perhaps because of the bird's sharp call, a popular saying has arisen that "when the cuckoo sings, its blood flows."

❖

BOKUSUI

墨 水

Died on the twenty-ninth day of November, 1914
at the age of forty

A parting word?	*Jisei nado*
The melting snow	*zansetsu ni ka mo*
is odorless.	*nakarikeri*

BUFU

蕪 風

Died on the twenty-fourth day of the seventh month, 1792

Oh, I don't care	*Ā mama yo*
where autumn clouds	*izuku e chiro to*
are drifting to.	*aki no kumo*

BUNZAN

蚊 山

Died on the fourteenth day of the first month, 1787

I crossed from last
year to the new—
today's the limit.

Shōgatsu no
toshi koe kyō o
kagiri nari

❖

BUSON

蕉　村

Died on the twenty-fifth day of the twelfth month, 1783
at the age of sixty-eight

Of late the nights
are dawning
plum-blossom white.

Shiraume ni
akaru yo bakari to
narinikeri

Buson was one of Japan's greatest poets. His poetry influenced
modern haiku even more, perhaps, than that of Basho. The
poetry of Buson, who was also a talented painter, is full of
color and fine details.

About a month before his death, Buson is said to have gone
picking mushrooms in the hills, and on his return he fell ill.
On the twenty-fourth day of the twelfth month, on the
evening of his death, he called his disciple Gekkei, gave him
a brush, and asked him to write down three poems. The
image of a nightingale appears in the first two poems, and in
the third that of a plum. Both images are associated with the
late winter and early spring season.

CHIBOKU

知 木

Died on the twenty-eighth day of the fifth month, 1740
at the age of forty-four

The running stream
is cool—the pebbles
underfoot.

Yuku mizu to
tomo ni suzushiku
ishi kawa ya

CHIKURO

竹 露

Died on the twenty-third day of March, 1895
at the age of seventy-one

Butterflies in flight:
the journey's end—
Suma Akashi.

Chō tobu ya
miateshi tabi wa
Suma Akashi

Suma is a region of Kobe along the coast of Osaka Bay;
Akashi is a nearby city and the name of a strait opening into
the bay. The area is noted for its beautiful scenery.

CHINE

千 子

*Died on the fifteenth day of the fifth month, 1688
at the age of about twenty-eight*

It lights up	*Moeyasuku*
as lightly as it fades:	*mata kieyasuki*
a firefly.	*hotaru kana*

Chine was the sister of Mukai Kyorai (1651–1704), a disciple
and friend of Basho's. After Chine's death Kyorai wrote:

Sadly I see	*Te no ue ni*
the light fade on my palm:	*kanashiku kiyuru*
a firefly.	*hotaru kana*

The *Kyoraisho* (Writings of Kyorai, 1775) tells us that
shortly after Chine's death, Kyorai aired out her summer
wardrobe. Just at that time he received a poem that was
written in his sister's memory by Basho:

Airing out the robe	*Naki hito no*
of one who is no more:	*kosode mo imaya*
autumn cleaning.	*doyōboshi*

❖

CHIRI

千 里

*Died on the eighteenth day of the seventh month, 1716
at the age of sixty-nine*

First crops:	*Shimmai ya*
my pillow fluffed up high,	*chagayu kuratte*
I gulp down rice and tea.	*takamakura*

Chiri died in the autumn, during the rice harvest. *Shimmai,*
"new rice," is considered tastier than rice stored from the
previous harvest. In the past the Japanese would bring the
firstfruits of the harvest to the temples.

Chagayu is a gruel made from rice, green tea, and salt.
Takamakura, "high pillow," refers metaphorically to peaceful
sleep, free from the worries of this world.

❖

CHIRI

千 里

*Died on the seventeenth day of September, 1917
at the age of sixteen*

Feast of the Dead—	*Bon wa itsu made*
how long can it go on?	*tsuzuku koto yara*
lanterns hung up high.	*takatōro*

It would seem that by "lanterns hung up high" *(takatōro)* the poet had in mind the lights which are hung in the doorway during the Bon Festival, which would have taken place some months before her death.

❖

CHIRIN

智 輪

Died on the twenty-fourth day of the twelfth month, 1794
at the age of sixty

In earth and sky	*Ametsuchi ni*
no grain of dust—	*chiri naki yuki no*
snow on the foothills.	*fumoto kana*

Chiri naki means "without dust." The poem is evidently a play on words using the poet's name: *Chirin naki* would mean "without Chirin."

❖

CHIYOJO

千 代 女

Died on the nineteenth day of the first month, 1746
past the age of twenty

A fawn frolics	*No ni asobu*
in the field—I put on my new	*kanoko mo ureshi*
spring robe.	*kisohajime*

Kisohajime refers to fresh clothes worn on New Year's Day, which fell around the beginning of spring when the lunar calendar was used. The Japanese, principally women and children, wear new kimonos made especially for the occasion. Chiyojo makes a pun on the word *kanoko,* which signifies literally a fawn but also refers to a particular white-spotted tie-dyed pattern on a kimono, perhaps on the one she was wearing that year.

❖

CHIYONI

千 代 尼

*Died on the eighth day of the ninth month, 1775
at the age of seventy-three*

I saw the moon as well	*Tsuki mo mite*
and now, world,	*ware wa kono yo o*
"truly yours . . ."	*kashiku kana*

Chiyoni, one of the best-known women haiku poets, became a Buddhist nun at the age of fifty-two. In her death poem she creates a metaphor of life as a letter. *Kashiku* is a phrase used by women to end their letters.

❖

CHOGO

朝　伍

*Died on the third day of the ninth month, 1806
at the age of forty-five*

I long for people—   *Hito koishi*
then again I loathe them: *hito mutsukashishi*
end of autumn.   *aki no kure*

❖

CHOHA

超　波

*Died in 1740
at the age of thirty-six*

A raging sea   *Araumi e*
thrown from the deck—   *fune kara nageru*
a block of ice.   *kōri kana*

❖

CHOKO

暢　好

Died on the second day of the tenth month, 1731
at the age of forty-six

This final scene I'll not see	*Sue ikki*
to the end—my dream	*mi hatenu yume no*
is fraying.	*hotsure kana*

Choko lived through the spring, summer, and autumn of his last year, dying on the second day of winter. One can also understand "this final scene" in the light of one belief, according to which man is given fifty years to live. Choko missed achieving his allotted life-span by four years.

❖

CHORA

蝶　羅

Died on the sixth day of the fifth month, 1776
at the age of fifty-four

"Paradise,"	*Gokuraku to*
I murmur, sleeping	*iute neburu ya*
in my netted tent.	*kaya no uchi*

After his death, Chora's wife, Motojo, answered with a poem of mourning:

The drone of the mosquitoes
round the netting, too,
is sad.

Ka no koe mo
kanashiki kaya no
atari kana

Chora died in summer, when netting is hung down from the ceiling to form a kind of chamber, as protection from mosquitoes and flies.

❖

CHORI

登 里

Died on the nineteenth day of the tenth month, 1778
at the age of thirty-nine

Leaves never fall
in vain—from all around
bells tolling.

Uso ni chiru
ha mo nashi yomo no
kane no koe

❖

CHOSHI

蝶 之

Died on the twenty-fifth day of the eighth month, 1768
at the age of fifty-one

On its way west
to paradise—
migrating bird.

Gokuraku no
michi o nishi e to
wataridori

❖

CHOSUI

鳥　酔

Died on the fourth day of the fourth month, 1769
at the age of sixty-nine

I wait, white clouds
and dark clouds passing—
a cuckoo cries.

Koki usuki
kumo o machiete
hototogisu

❖

CHOWA

調　和

Died on the seventeenth day of the tenth month, 1715
at the age of seventy-eight

This is one poem
people won't dispute—
the winds of winter.

Kono ikku
shūgihan nashi
kogarashi no

❖

DAIBAI

大　梅

*Died on the twenty-ninth day of the fifth month, 1841
at the age of seventy*

My seventy years—a withered
pampas tail and all around it
iris blooming.

*Nanajū ya
ayame no naka no
kareobana*

The *ayame* is a species of iris which grows on the hillsides and in the fields of Japan, to a height of from thirty to fifty centimeters. Its leaves are long and narrow, its flowers purple, the base of its petals yellow.

Obana, "tail plant" (from *kareobana*) is the name of the Japanese pampas grass, which is also called *susuki.* This plant, the head of which resembles the bushy tail of an animal, grows all over the hills and fields of Japan and is used for making straw roofs, sacks, brooms, and mats. It provides food for farm animals, and a fever-abating medicine is made from it.

Daibai died in summer, when the *ayame* blossoms. He likens his old age to a withered pampas plant *(kareobana),* though the pampas itself dies in winter.

Daibai was originally a scholar of Chinese literature. When he began to devote himself to haiku, his colleagues complained to him, "Among those of us who studied together, one has become a writer of *kyoka* and one a writer of popular romances. And now you, Daibai, want to be a haiku poet?" Daibai answered his critics with a verse:

You cannot tell	*Fugu kuwanu*
its taste to him	*hito ni wa iwaji*
who never tasted blowfish.	*fugu no aji*

The blowfish *(fugu)* is considered a delicacy, but preparing it requires considerable skill. If the poison in the fish's body is not successfully removed, it can cause death.

❖

DOHAKU

道 伯

Died in 1675

Cargoless,	*Tsumimono ya*
bound heavenward,	*nakute jōdo e*
ship of the moon.	*tsuki no fune*

There is a play on words in the original. *Tsumi* can mean "sin" as well as "loading." The first phrase could thus be rendered "sinless."

Tsuki no fune means, as translated, "ship of the moon," but the phrase can also be understood as "ship beneath the moon."

❖

DONSUI

呑　水

Died on the fourth day of the tenth month, 1729

Lotus seeds in ten
directions jumping
playfully.

Hasu no mi no
tonde jippō ni
asobikeri

The lotus *(hasu)* is a perennial broad-leaved water plant found
in ponds and marshes. In summer it blossoms white and
scarlet and gives off a strong scent. For three days the lotus
flower opens at sunrise and closes in the afternoon, withering
on the fourth day. The lotus is one of the symbols of Bud-
dhism, and tradition pictures the Pure Land in the West as
a lotus-covered lake. The journey to the world of the dead
is sometimes pictured as a boat trip across such a lake.

❖

ENRYO

燕　凌

Died on the fifteenth day of the seventh month, 1855
at the age of fifty-five

Autumn waters	*Yoizame no*
of this world wake me	*kore ya konoyo no*
from my drunkenness.	*aki no mizu*

One Japanese custom is to give water known as *shinimizu,* "death water," to the dying. The practice is not only a means of relieving the parched lips of the dying person: he is always given the water by a close relative or a good friend, and the waters often come from a particular source. This ancient custom may have had its beginnings in the belief that water binds the soul of the dying to the world it is trying to leave.

   In Enryo's poem, the last waters of this world are "autumn waters" *(aki no mizu),* for the poet died early in this season. The waters waken the dying person from the intoxications of his life and sober him from the illusions of existence.

❖

ENSEI

延 清

*Died on the sixteenth day of the fifth month, 1725
at the age of sixty-nine*

A parting gift to my body:	*Itsu totemo*
just when it wishes,	*iki hikitoru ga*
I'll breathe my last.	*mi no seibo*

In the last days of the old year the Japanese customarily send gifts known as *seibo* to their friends and relatives, thanking them for kindnesses bestowed throughout the year. Ensei thanks his body for services rendered during his life, and as a "parting gift," he is ready to rid it of the soul whenever it wishes.

❖

ENSETSU

燕　説

Died on the nineteenth day of the ninth month, 1743
at the age of seventy-three

Autumn gust:	*Kono kai ni*
I have no further business	*ni-do to yō nashi*
in this world.	*aki no kaze*

Ensetsu grew up in a Zen Buddhist temple and in his later years served as a priest. To the haiku written before his death he attached, as was the custom among Zen monks, a death poem in Chinese as well:

Many things befell me as I followed Buddha
Three and seventy years.
What is death?
Freely, from my own true self,
Ho! Ho!

"Ho!" is a translation of *totsu,* a cry of enlightenment.
Ensetsu was very much attached to his haiku master, Rosen

(p. 266), with whom he roamed all over Japan. When Ensetsu heard of his master's having fallen ill, he hastened to his side, though he himself was suffering from severe stomach pains. From the day Rosen died, Ensetsu's disease worsened, and he survived his master less than a month.

❖

ENSHI

燕 枝

*Died on the twelfth day of February, 1900
at the age of sixty-three*

All moving things	*Ugoku mono*
come to an end:	*owari arikeri*
a knotty willow.	*kobu yanagi*

Kobu means "swelling" and can refer to a knot in the wood of the tree. The same word applies, however, to the tumors of diseases afflicting man.

❖

FUFU

浮 風

*Died on the seventeenth day of the fifth month, 1762
at the age of sixty-one*

My companion in the skies of death, a cuckoo.	*Tsure mo ari imawa no sora no hototogisu*

❖

FUJO

風　状

*Died on the twenty-seventh day of the eighth month, 1764
at the age of fifty-two*

Rise, let us go— along the path lies the clear dew.	*Okiagari yukamuzu michi no tsuyu kiyoshi*

❖

FUKAKU

不　角

*Died on the twenty-first day of the sixth month, 1753
at the age of ninety-two*

Empty cicada shell: as we come we go back naked.	*Utsu semi wa moto no hadaka ni modorikeri*

The larva of the cicada *(semi)* stays underground a number of years. In summer it emerges from the ground, sheds its armored skin, and unfolds its wings. The hard cicada shells cling to tree trunks or lie on the ground. The shell is not actually the cicada's corpse, but the cicada that emerges from it, flutters here and there, and utters shrill cries is destined to die within a few days.

❖

FUKYU

普 求

*Died on the twenty-first day of the seventh month, 1771
at the age of seventy-nine*

A bright and pleasant
autumn day to make
death's journey.

*Kokochiyoshi
aki no hiyori o
shide no tabi*

❖

FUSEN

賦 泉

*Died on the twenty-ninth day of the eleventh month, 1777
at the age of fifty-seven*

Today, then, is the day
the melting snowman
is a real man.

*Kyō to iu
kyō zo makoto no
yukibotoke*

Fusen died in the depth of winter, and the image of a man melting like a snowman is a seasonal one.

Yukibotoke (*yuki*, snow; *botoke*, from *hotoke*, Buddha) is one term for "snowman" in Japanese; however, the word *yukidaruma*, "Daruma of snow," is more popular. Snowmen are built to represent the Indian monk Daruma (Skt., Bodhidharma), who, according to tradition, wandered to China in 520 A.D. and founded there the Zen Buddhist sect. The expression *yukibotoke* has an additional meaning, for *hotoke* is a term used by the Japanese for any person who has died. The image is not only seasonal, but one of transience.

❖

FUSO

不 争

Died on the eleventh day of the fourth month, 1886
at the age of forty-seven

Upon the lotus flower	*Asatsuyu no*
morning dew is	*usura kiekeri*
thinning out.	*hasu no hana*

❖

FUWA

風 和

Died in the second month, 1712

The earth is fragrant	*Ume chirishi*
with plum petals falling	*nioi no tsuchi o*
on my way home.	*kokyō e zo*

Fuwa, a resident of Yamagata, in northern Japan, died away from home in Kyoto in the plum-blossom season. In the cold northern regions of Japan, the plum blossoms later than elsewhere in the country.

 ⸳ *Kokyo,* which refers to one's birthplace, also suggests the "place" from which man comes and to which he returns.

❖

GAKI

我　鬼

Died on the twenty-fourth day of July, 1927
at the age of thirty-six

One spot, alone,	*Mizubana ya*
left glowing in the dark:	*hana no saki dake*
my snotty nose.	*kure nokoru*

Gaki, better known by his real name, Akutagawa Ryunosuke, prefaced his poem with the words "laughing at myself." He gave the poem to his aunt on the night of July twenty-third and asked her to deliver it the next morning to the family doctor, who was himself a haiku poet. The same night Akutagawa killed himself by drinking poison.

Akutagawa was one of Japan's greatest modern authors.

A short time after his birth his mother became insane, which cast a heavy shadow on his life. One of his first stories, entitled *Hana* (Nose), won much praise from the writer Natsume Soseki (1867–1916) and put Akutagawa well into the literary scene of his age.

❖

GANSAN

翫 山

Died in 1895
at the age of eighty-one

Blow if you will,
fall wind—the flowers
have all faded.

Fukaba fuke
hana wa sunda zo
aki no kaze

❖

GAZEN

瓦 全

Died on the twenty-seventh day of the eleventh month, 1825
at the age of eighty-two

I lean against
the stove and lo!
eternity.

Motaretaru
kotatsu sunawachi
jakkōdo

A *kotatsu* is a low table under which a heating device is placed and over which a large padded tablecloth is spread. People sit on cushions and stretch their legs beneath the table, gathering the edge of the cloth around the lower part of their bodies.

Jakkodo means "peaceful land of eternal light." It is another of the many names given by Buddhists to the next life or to the state of enlightenment.

Gazen died in the middle of winter. Are we to picture death coming instantly to a man, as if one moment he may be leaning on the *kotatsu* warming his bones, and the next he finds himself in "eternity"? It is perhaps preferable to read the poem as an image of one place and time. Gazen's eighty-two years must have taught him that this world of the senses and the realm of the absolute are found wherever one sees them.

❖

GENGEN'ICHI

玄 々 一

Died on the twenty-fifth day of the eighth month, 1804
at the age of sixty-three

Morning glory	*Asagao ya*
even though you wither	*shibomeba mata no*
dawn will break anew.	*asaborake*

Gengen'ichi lost his sight in childhood; his wife and children later helped him to read and write. Might the blind poet have touched the flower with his hands and sensed the tragedy of its fleeting life, consoling it with the "dawn" of another flower?

The morning glory *(asagao)* is a climbing plant that blooms around August in various colors. The flower opens at dawn and wilts in the afternoon of the same day; hence its name in Japanese—"morning face." Because of its short blooming time, the morning glory is considered a symbol of transience. Its blossoming season comes to an end at the beginning of autumn, the season in which Gengen'ichi died.

❖

GENSHO

原　松

Died on the fifth day of the first month, 1742
at the age of fifty-eight

A graveyard:	*Hakahara ya*
autumn fireflies	*aki no hotaru no*
two or three.	*futatsu mitsu*

One source gives the following background to this poem:

A Zen monk from Myoshinji temple in Kyoto came to Gensho with a picture of a skull that he had painted and asked the monk to compose a poem for it.

On the fifth day of the first month, 1742, Gensho wrote [the poem above]. When he finished, he put down his brush and died. . . . His followers took this to be his death poem.[2]

Summer is the season for fireflies *(hotaru)* but even during autumn nights the light of a few late fireflies can be seen flickering here and there.

❖

GETSUREI

月 嶺

*Died on the twenty-ninth day of January, 1919
at the age of forty*

Stumble,	*Shirayuki ni*
fall,	*suberi-ochikeri*
slide down the snow slope.	*masshigura*

❖

GIMEI

祇 名

*Died on the fourth day of the tenth month, 1748
at the age of fifty-one*

Illness lingers on and on	*Yami yamishi*
till over Basho's withered field,	*hate ya okina no*
the moon.	*kareno-zuki*

This death poem borrows the metaphor found in the poem

by Basho (p. 143), whom Gimei calls *okina,* "the old one." It may be that Gimei secretly expected to leave the world on the anniversary of Basho's death (the twelfth day of the tenth month), but death overtook him eight days early.

"Withered field" *(kareno)* is an image of winter, the season in which both poets died.

❖

GINKA

吟 霞

Died on the first day of the eighth month, 1784
at the age of sixty-one

I leap from depths	*Shakusen no*
of debt into the skies:	*fuchi kara tenjō*
autumn of the dragon.	*tatsu no aki*

The year 1784, in the autumn of which Ginka died, was the year of the dragon, one of the twelve signs of the Oriental zodiac. There is a popular belief that the dragon, living in the depths of the sea, rises on a column of clouds and rain to the sky at the end of its life. We may understand from this poem that its author had many debts, and that he regarded his death, with a touch of humor, as a perfect solution to his financial worries.

❖

GINKO

銀 甲

Died on the nineteenth day of the first month, 1790
at the age of seventy-three

See—	*Okuretari*
see how the spring slush melts away	*awayuki kienu*
and I still here . . .	*korewa korewa*

If the day of Ginko's death is computed by the solar calendar,
it appears that he died in the beginning of March. By that
time the snow is melting in the southern parts of Japan.

❖

GITOKU

祇 徳

Died on the twenty-fourth day of the eleventh month, 1754
at the age of fifty-three

Clear sky—	*Sora saete*
the way I came by once	*moto kishi michi o*
I now go back by.	*kaeru nari*

❖

GOCHU

吾 仲

Died on the thirtieth day of the ninth month, 1733

This is what I think:	*Omou koto*
the sky has ended—	*sora no shimai ya*
end of the ninth month.	*kugatsujin*

By the old calendar, the thirtieth day (the last day) of the ninth month was the last day of autumn.

❖

GODO

梧 堂

Died in 1801

Chrysanthemums were yellow	*Shiragiku mo*
or were white	*kigiku mo shimo o*
until the frost.	*ichigo kana*

The chrysanthemum (*kiku;* in this poem in the forms *shiragiku,* white chrysanthemum, and *kigiku,* yellow chrysanthemum) is common throughout Japan, and the Japanese consider it a symbol of their culture. By an ancient Oriental tradition, powder made from the petals of this flower is both a remedy for illness and a talisman for long life. There are many kinds of chrysanthemums in Japan, both domesticated and wild, with very large and very small blossoms of various colors. People make a practice of visiting gardens to enjoy the sight of the blooming flowers. In haiku, "chrysanthemum" usually figures as a season word for autumn.

❖

GOFU

梧　風

Died on the eighteenth day of the eighth month, 1771
at the age of thirty-eight

I have not yet grown weary	*Mada akanu*
of this world—where do	*yo o akikaze no*
fall breezes blow?	*yukue kana*

There is a play on words in this poem. *Aki* is a form of the verb *aku*, "to grow weary." *Aki* also means "autumn." *Kaze* means "wind," so *akikaze* may mean "autumn wind" or "weary winds."

❖

GOHEI

五　瓶

Died on the second day of the second month, 1808
at the age of sixty-two or sixty-three

The second month:	*Ume wa saku*
plum blossoms filling out—	*ware wa chiriyuku*
I fade away.	*kisaragi ya*

❖

GOHEI

五　瓶

Died on the seventh day of the seventh month, 1819

A lone paulownia leaf	*Aki ya ima*
falls through	*kiyoshi to kiri no*
pure autumn air.	*hito-ha chiru*

The paulownia *(kiri)* is a tree with large purple flowers, a member of the figwort family. A "lone paulownia leaf" appears in ancient Chinese poetry as a seasonal image for the first part of autumn. Even without the aid of autumn winds, the large leaves of the paulownia tree fall one by one. This sight suggests the beginning of autumn and the oncoming end of life.

❖

GOKEI

吾 桂

*Died on the twenty-seventh day of the eighth month, 1769
at the age of fifty-three*

Fields dying off:	*Kiete yuku*
the underside of grasses frozen	*no mo uragare no*
hour of my death.	*hotoke kana*

In this poem the image of man's death is interwoven into a
scene from nature at the end of autumn. *Uragare,* a season
word for autumn, describes field grass frozen on the side not
exposed to the sun.

❖

GOSEN

後 川

Died in winter, 1799

Spring will meet this year	*Toshi no uchi no*
before it's out	*haru ni mo aenu*
but as for me . . .	*inochi kana*

Although by the old calendar spring usually began on New
Year's Day or shortly thereafter, there were years in which

it began before the new year, and this was evidently the case in the year Gosen died. Though fate cut him off before the end of the year, he might have remained alive till the first day of spring within the old year. According to old sources, however, he died during winter.

❖

GOSHI

五　始

Died on the thirteenth day of the ninth month, 1775
at the age of sixty-six

Returning thanks	*Shōgai no*
for life, I turn back and bow	*oreigaeshi ya*
eastward.	*higashi muki*

To thank the living for kindnesses received during life, the dying poet turns toward the east before starting westward, the direction of paradise.

❖

GOSHU

五　株

Died on the twenty-eighth day of the sixth month, 1788
at the age of sixty-six

Disgusted with	*Itou yo o*
the world, I withdraw	*noita kokoro zo*
into the net.	*kaya no naka*

Goshu died in summer, when the Japanese hang netting over their bedding as protection from flies and mosquitoes.

❖

GOSHUKU

互 夙

Died in 1888(?)

A cuckoo cries	*Kagiri naku*
the end—clouds	*hototogisu nari*
on a summer morn.	*asagumori*

This poem is inscribed on Goshuku's gravestone, which lies in a temple in Kyoto. The date of his death is uncertain, but it is known that the tombstone was erected in April 1888.

❖

GOZAN

梧 山

Died on the second day of the third month, 1733
at the age of thirty-eight

Blossoms scent the air	*Ka ya hiraki*
a carefree birdsong	*nori toku tori no*
echoes truth.	*kirabiyaka*

This haiku is a *kaibun* poem, a palindrome in which the sequence of syllables is identical whether the poem is read from the beginning or from the end. Such a form was popular in Japanese poetry during the eighteenth and nineteenth centuries.

One source has this to say about Gozan's death:

> The evening Gozan died there were still several blossoms left on the plum tree outside his window. From time to time an owl came to rest in the tree, calling, *"ho, ho."* Said Gozan, "My life is over. . . ." He took up his brush and wrote his death poem.[3]

The syllable *ho* is the Chinese-derived pronunciation of the character signifying "law," or "Buddha's doctrine." Gozan uses the same character with its Japanese pronunciation, *nori,* in his poem.

❖

GOZAN

吾 山

*Died on the seventeenth day of the twelfth month, 1789
at the age of seventy-one*

The snow of yesterday	*Hana to mishi*
that fell like cherry petals	*yuki wa kinō zo*
is water once again.	*moto no mizu*

Only *hana,* "flower," is mentioned in the poem, but in the tradition of haiku this word refers to cherry blossoms. In the earliest Japanese literature, falling cherry blossoms are linked with falling snow. The two images are not only visually similar, but they share the metaphorical meaning of transience as well. The cherry tree blooms for a week only, and spring snows melt almost immediately upon touching the ground.

❖

HAKUEN

白　猿

*Died on the twenty-ninth day of the tenth month, 1806
at the age of sixty-six*

I wonder where	*Kogarashi ni*
the winds of winter	*ame motsu kumo no*
drive the rainclouds . . .	*yukue kana*

❖

HAKUEN

白 猿

Died on the twenty-third day of the third month, 1859
at the age of seventy

What is it but a dream?   *Ā yume da*
The blossoming as well   *hana no tomari mo*
lasts only seven cycles.   *nana-meguri*

Hakuen died in the spring during the cherry-blossom season.
"Seven cycles" *(mana-meguri)* refers to the seven-day life of the
blossom, and the seven cycles of the poet are, apparently, the
seven decades of his life.

❖

HAKUJUBO

白 寿 坊

Died on the sixteenth day of the sixth month, 1817

My heart serene,   *Nishi no sora e*
I set out   *kokoro suzushiki*
for the western skies.   *kadode kana*

❖

HAKUKIN

白 芹

*Died on the twenty-first day of the tenth month, 1817
at the age of sixty-two*

Pampas grass, all dry	*Mizu ya sora*
crumbles apart	*hodokete shimau*
water and sky . . .	*karesusuki*

Susuki is synonymous with *obana,* both referring to Japanese pampas grass (see p. 157). *Karesusuki* means "withered pampas grass."

❖

HAKUNI

白 尼

*Died on the ninth day of the eighth month, 1792
at the age of eighty-four*

To a melody of prayer	*Shōmyō ni*
disappears the moon—	*tsuki mo kietaru*
my place of rest.	*makura kana*

Shomyo is one of the names given to the prayer *Namu Amida Butsu* (lit., I put my trust in Amida Buddha), which is recited by many Buddhists at the hour of death in the belief that they will be reborn in the Pure Land in the West.

❖

HAKURIN

白　隣

Died on the third day of October, 1897
at the age of sixty-eight

Well, then, let's follow
the peal of bells to the
yonder shore.

Iza yukan
higan no kane no
ato ōte

Hakurin died shortly after the equinox *(higan)* of autumn. On that day the Japanese hold ceremonies to commemorate the Buddha's death, visit temples, and lay flowers on the graves of their ancestors.

Higan means literally "the other shore" and as such indicates the passage from the world of illusion to that of truth.

❖

HAKURO

白　露

Died on the nineteenth day of the twelfth month, 1766

An ailing mallard
falls through the chilly night
and teeters off.

Yamu kari no
yosamu ni orite
obotsukana

In the autumn of 1690, Basho stayed in the town of Katata on Lake Biwa. There he fell ill, and wrote:

An ailing mallard	*Yamu kari no*
falls through the cold of night—	*yosamu ni ochite*
my slumber on a journey.	*tabine kana*

Clearly, Hakuro had Basho's poem in mind when he wrote his death poem.

Kari is a general name for different kinds of wild ducks, which are a common feature of Japanese scenery during autumn and winter. In autumn, wild ducks fly in from northern countries in V-shaped flocks. They winter beside lakes and marshes, and can be seen sleeping on the surface of water at night. The call of wild ducks echoes in the air all winter long until they return north at the beginning of spring.

❖

HAKUSAI

白 歳

*Died on the second day of the ninth month, 1792
at the age of seventy-four*

Farewell—and though there be	*Saraba saraba*
no budding in the spring,	*hana mo momiji mo*
no autumn withering—all is well.	*naki zo yoki*

❖

HAKUSEN

伯　先

*Died on the twenty-third day of the eighth month, 1820
at the age of sixty-five*

Oh, morning glory,
five and sixty years—
I too pass away.

*Asagao yo
musoji–itsu–tose
mi wa owaru*

❖

HAKUSETSU

白　雪

*Died on the seventh day of the sixth month, 1735
at the age of seventy-five*

At peace,
above my sickness
summer smolders.

*Anjin wa
yamai ga ue no
gokusho kana*

❖

HAKUTO

伯　兎

Died in 1727

Deutzia blossoms: *Unohana ya*
I, who rebuked the lazy,   *iken suru mi mo*
sleep late into the morning.   *asane-doki*

Unohana refers to the deutzia plant, a bush with white flowers.
It grows in the mountains, fields, and along garden fences
throughout Japan, its blossoms heralding the coming of
summer.

❖

HAMEI

巴　明

Died on the twenty-sixth day of the twelfth month, 1837
at the age of eighty-three

Man's end,   *Mi no hate wa*
a mound of gleaming bones: *shari no hikari ya*
a flowering and a fading.   *hanagokoro*

❖

HAMON

巴　紋

Died on the twenty-first day of the second month, 1804
at the age of fifty-eight

In stillness, I,	*Nodokasa ya*
light-bodied, set out for	*ware wa migaruki*
the other world.	*nori no tabi*

❖

HANKAI

半 海

Died on the fourth day of January, 1882
at the age of seventy-six

The year is ending:	*Yuku toshi no*
I have not left my heart	*kokoro-nokori wa*
behind.	*nakarikeri*

The expression *yuku toshi,* "the passing year," refers to the last days of December. The metaphor "I have not left my heart / behind," familiar to Western readers, suggests that there is no regret or sorrow over the past.

❖

HANRI

畔 李

Died on the twelfth day of the fifth month, 1835
at the age of seventy-one

My life:	Isshō no
echoes of a clucking tongue	shitauchi hibiku
above pure waters.	shimizu kana

Shitauchi (clucking of the tongue) refers to the sound a person makes with his tongue signifying regret over failures in the past and resignation to the unavoidable.

Shimizu, "pure water," calls to mind the water of streams breaking out of the ground in summer after the rainy season. But there may be, as well, a suggestion of *shinimizu,* the water given by Japanese to the dying.

❖

HOGYOKU

豊 玉

Died on the eleventh day of the fifth month, 1869
at the age of thirty-five

Quick sounds	Tatakarete
of chopping echo	oto no hibikishi
New Year's herbs.	nazuna kana

Hogyoku (Hijikata Saizo) was an officer in the shogunate army that was defeated by the imperial forces during the Meiji Restoration. He retreated with the remnants of his army to the island of Hokkaido in the north. There, mounted on a horse and with sword drawn, he sallied forth ahead of his soldiers into a lost battle against the emperor's forces. He was wounded by an enemy bullet and fell from his horse. Two of his close friends carried him to a shack in a grove of pine trees, and there he died in the arms of his companions. When they took the uniform off his body, they found, pressed against his back, the bloodied scroll of paper on which his death poem was written.

Nazuna is an herb eaten on the seventh day of the new year.

❖

HOKUSAI

北 斎

*Died on the twelfth day of the fourth month, 1849
at the age of ninety*

Now as a spirit	*Hitodama de*
I shall roam	*yuku kisan ja*
the summer fields.	*natsu no hara*

Hokusai was one of Japan's greatest artists. His colorful paintings of Edo's street life are among the best made in *ukiyoe* style, and his series of thirty-seven views of Mount Fuji brought him fame falling little short of that of the mountain itself.

Hitodama (lit., man-ball) refers to the ghost or spirit of the dead. Various beliefs about *hitodama* have been held in Japan—that the spirit leaves the body at the moment of death in the form of a pale blue ball of fire floating in the air, that it stays close to the home of the deceased for forty-nine days after death, and that ghosts hover over cemeteries.

❖

HOKUSHI

北 枝

Died on the twelfth day of the eighth month, 1718

I write, erase, rewrite,	*Kaite mitari*
erase again, and then	*keshitari hate wa*
a poppy blooms.	*keshi no hana*

Hokushi's death poem is built around a pun. *Keshi* means "to erase" as well as "poppy," so the poem may be read, "I write, erase, rewrite, / erase again, and then / a flower erases." However it is read, the poem's intent remains the same—that nature eventually overwhelms culture. The poppy blooms in Japan at the beginning of summer, the season in which Hokushi died.

Hokushi, a sword-sharpener, learned to write haiku from Basho. He would not hesitate to suggest changes in his teacher's poems, and Basho praised him for his helpful criticism.

It is said that Hokushi was extremely poor, but of a cheerful disposition. When his house burned down, he wrote:

Gone up in flames—	*Yakenikeri*
but look, the flowers droop	*saredomo hana wa*
unknowing.	*chirisumashi*

Hokushi had a weakness for liquor and used to ask for wine from his neighbor, the poet Joryu. Hokushi and his elder brother Bokudo, himself a poet, were famous for their ability to sleep while sitting and were accordingly styled "champion dozers."

❖

HOKUSO

北 窓

Died on the sixth day of the sixth month, 1790

O sacred spirit	*Shōryō ni*
let us set out	*iza tsuredatan*
for the western skies.	*nishi no sora*

Shoryo alludes, apparently, to the spirit of Buddha. The same Chinese characters with the pronunciation *seirei* give the name for the Holy Spirit of Christianity.

❖

HOROKU

宝 六

Died on the eleventh day of April, 1878

Mountain temple:	*Yamadera ya*
far as the pillow where I lie	*makuramoto made*
the willow sheds its flowers.	*chiru yanagi*

❖

HOU

法 雨

Died on the first day of the first month, 1811
at the age of eighty-six

Encased by winter:	*Fuyugomori*
before long I'll	*tsui karazake to*
become dried salmon.	*narinikeri*

Fuyugomori means "winter confinement" or "hibernation."
In the northern parts of Japan, where winter snow piles
high, people shut themselves up in their houses in the depth
of winter.

The image of dried salmon *(karazake)* is not necessarily a
season word indicating winter. It may suggest the wrinkled
body of the eighty-six-year-old Hou.

❖

HOYU

方 由

Died at the end of the seventeenth century

Praise to the skies: *Namu ya sora*
alone in moonlit early dawn   *tada ariake no*
a cuckoo cries.   *hototogisu*

Namu stands for *Namu Amida Butsu,* the prayer to the Buddha Amida.

❖

HYAKKA

百　花

Died on the twentieth day of the second month, 1779
at the age of sixty-four

Late-blooming cherry: *Okufukaki*
wondrous workings   *hana no kokoro ya*
of a flower's mind.   *osozakura*

*　*　*　*

Winter ice   *Kōri toke*
melts into clean water—   *yuku mizu kiyoshi*
clear is my heart.   *mune kiyoshi*

Two death poems have been ascribed to Hyakka. Both cherry blossoms and melting ice are images of spring, the season in which the poet died.

❖

HYAKURI

百 里

Died on the twelfth day of the fifth month, 1727
at the age of sixty-two

When I die
what I shall see will be
the lustrous moon.

Shinite okite
suzushiki tsuki o
miru zo kashi

❖

ICHIMU

一 夢

Died on the twenty-first day of the ninth month, 1854
at the age of fifty-one

A broken dream—
where do they go
the butterflies?

Yume hitotsu
yaburete chō no
yukue kana

The poet's name is composed of the characters for "one"*(ichi)*
and "dream" *(mu)* in their Chinese-derived pronunciations.
In Ichimu's death poem the same characters appear in Japanese
word order and pronunciation (*yume,* dream; *hitotsu,* one).
The "broken dream" is that illusion whereby we ascribe
reality to a transient world. When life ends, the illusion of
one's individual being bursts, and with it disappears the sym-
bol of that being—one's name.

The butterfly *(cho)* appears in haiku of spring, summer, and autumn, but its season is in fact the flowering period of spring and early summer. The further autumn advances, the fewer butterflies become, and the paler their colors are. Ichimu died late in this season.

Were the butterflies a mere dream? In the writings of the Chinese philosopher Chuang-tzu, we find the following words:

> Chuang-tzu once dreamed he was a butterfly soaring on fluttering wings, content with himself and following his own desires. He knew not that he was Chuang-tzu. But suddenly he woke and found that he was most certainly Chuang-tzu. He no longer knew if he was a butterfly in Chuang-tzu's dream, or Chuang-tzu in the dream of a butterfly.

❖

ICHISHI

一 四

Died on the fourteenth day of the ninth month, 1746
at the age of thirty-eight

What do you understand?	*Nani satoru*
One sound,	*katsu to hitokoe*
the voice of autumn.	*aki no koe*

The poet's question, "What do you understand?" (or "Are

you enlightened?"), is evidently turned toward himself. In the original Japanese, he answers with the exclamation *katsu* —the sharp cry emitted by Zen masters or pupils at the moment of enlightenment. Ichishi expresses the substance of that enlightenment by means of "one sound" *(hitokoe),* the voice of a solitary autumn cicada, whose hours are numbered. The poet himself died at the end of autumn.

In haiku, the "voice of autumn" *(aki no koe)* does not necessarily refer to a particular sound. The blowing wind, the dripping rain, and other sounds of nature that pass through the autumn air grown heavy with sadness may all be voices of autumn. But it seems that the expression pertains here to the voice of the cicada, whose chorus of chirps dies away toward the end of the season.

❖

INSEKI

因 石

*Died on the twenty-eighth day of the third month, 1765
at the age of sixty-seven*

I give my name back	*Na mo kaesu*
as I step in	*hana no jōdo e*
this Eden of flowers.	*yado hairi*

It is a Buddhist custom to change the name of a deceased person.

❖

IPPU

一 風

Died on the twenty-fourth day of the fifth month, 1731
at the age of sixty-seven

Falling in the wind   *Chiriyuku ya*
a gust   *kaze ni tokiwa no*
of evergreen leaves.   *konoha ame*

The setting in Ippu's death poem is in the fall, but it is not
taken from nature, as evergreen trees do not shed their leaves.
The paradox seems to arise from man's wonder in the face
of death. As long as he is alive he sees himself as an "ever-
green," and the falling of leaves has no part in his world.
However, when the "death wind" blows. . . .

There may be a connection between the poet's pen name
(lit., one wind) and the wind in the poem.

❖

ISAIBO

以 哉 坊

Died on the twenty-ninth day of the eighth month, 1780
at the age of sixty-six

Though I tarry on the road   *Shi ni shibashi*
my master took, above us glows   *okurete mo michi no*
one moon.   *tsuki onaji*

Tanaka Gochikubo, Isaibo's haiku master, died a month or two before his pupil. Old sources give accounts of the stormy relationship between the two poets. One of Isaibo's poems, about the beauty of Matsushima Bay (Miyagi Prefecture), reads:

> Matsushima: *Matsushima ya*
> their knees tear *hiza de momikiru*
> the ship's mats. *fune no goza*

The image of passengers crowding to the side of the ship in order to feast their eyes on the view, their knees scraping the straw mats covering the deck, seemed coarse to Gochikubo, who suggested a less crude rendering:

> Matsushima: *Matsushima ya*
> at sight of you *keshiki ni momeru*
> the ship mats crumple. *fune no goza*

Isaibo refused the correction and had to leave Gochikubo's circle. Another person made peace between them. In honor of Isaibo's return to his favor, Gochikubo wrote a poem in which he suggests that the two of them "blunt their edges" and behave more "roundedly" with one another.

Isaibo responded with his own poem, about a plum tree raised in a greenhouse in order to hasten its blossoming. This poem did not please Gochikubo, perhaps because Isaibo may have meant that he was being forced to mature as a poet in an unnatural way. Once again, Isaibo had to quit the company for a time.

In spite of the rivalry between the two, or perhaps because

of it, it would seem that Isaibo was fond of Gochikubo. The "road" in Isaibo's death poem is the road from life to death taken by both master and pupil, and the "one moon" is a symbol of the perfect unity which underlies this world of many changes.

❖

ISAN

伊　珊

Died in 1698

For not honoring my parents	*Isshō oya ni*
while I lived, in my last hour	*kō o nasazaru koto o*
I feel remorse.	*matsugo ni kuite*

* * * *

The autumn hues	*Sakazuki ni*
of knotweed seem	*nite inutade no*
like cups of wine.	*momiji kana*

Isan, who was apparently one of Basho's pupils, left two death poems. The first deals with the highest commandment of Confucian doctrine—honor for one's parents. It seems that this verse, which lacks the proper form (the original has twenty-four syllables) and poetic content, was uttered more by Isan the son than by Isan the poet.

The connection between the first and the second poems is not clear. One may, perhaps, conjecture as to the personal significance in the second, but it is just as well to see it as an image from nature. The plant referred to is an annual wild grass *(Poligonum blumei)* which grows to a height of about thirty centimeters and has long sharp-edged leaves. The plant is not used by man, and is not considered exceptionally beautiful (as is indicated by its Japanese name, *inutade,* lit., dog weed). The plant's sheaf-like, petalless yellow and red flowers start blooming about June and continue to the end of autumn.

❖

ISSA

一 茶

Died on the nineteenth day of the eleventh month, 1827
at the age of sixty-five

What matter if I live on—	*Ā mama yo*
a tortoise lives	*ikite mo kame no*
a hundred times as long.	*hyaku-bu ichi*

*   *   *   *

From one basin	*Tarai kara*
to another—	*tarai ni utsuru*
stuff and nonsense.	*chimpunkan*

Issa is considered one of Japan's greatest haiku poets. Among the common people of Japan he is perhaps loved more than any other poet, because of the many vicissitudes of his life, and because of the human simplicity of his poetry. Accounts of Issa's death do not indicate that he wrote a death poem; these two poems are held to be his death poems by popular tradition.

An ancient Oriental belief features the tortoise as a symbol of long life, ascribing to it a life of ten thousand years. Should man live to be one hundred, his life would be no more than a hundredth part of the life of this shell-covered creature that drags its tail in the mud. Why then should a man ask for another year, a month, or a day?

The word *tarai* in the second poem means "tub" or "basin." The reference is perhaps to the basins for cleaning newborn babies and cleansing the dead. The life of man is no more than gibberish (*chimpunkan* means, in colloquial speech, the unintelligible sounds of a foreign language) that begins in the cradle and ends in the grave.

❖

ISSHO

一 笑

Died on the sixth day of the twelfth month, 1688
at the age of thirty-six

From deep in my heart	*Kokoro kara*
how beautiful the snow	*yuki utsukushi ya*
clouds in the west.	*nishi no kumo*

The death of Issho is described in one source:

Issho, who lived in the city of Kanazawa, loved haiku.
When Basho passed through Kanazawa on a journey,
Issho wanted very much to lodge him in his home, but
that very year Issho had fallen deathly ill and knew his
end was near. It was the thirteenth year after his father's
death, and Issho decided to compose thirteen *kasen*
[thirty-six-verse *renga*] in memory of his father. His
friends tried to prevent this undertaking, saying, "Your
breathing is not regular. Who knows what will happen
to you after you have finished the thirteen poems?"
But Issho replied, "Even if I die, I will not be sorry."
After five poems Issho's breathing became heavy, and
he could hardly hold his brush. In spite of this he held on
and composed the other eight. When he had finished his
task, his eyes shone with joy and he announced, "With
these poems close to my body, I have nothing to regret."
As his eyelids grew heavier, he closed them and said
[the poem above]. He looked like a man who had been
freed from the chains of life and whose soul was pure.
In the autumn of the year following Issho's death, Basho
wrote a poem of lamentation in his memory: "Move,
O tomb / the sound of my weeping / is the wind of
autumn [*Tsuka mo ugoke / waga naku koe wa / aki no
kaze*].[4]

Issho's phrase "from deep in my heart" *(kokoro kara)* is
an expression rarely encountered in haiku. But death poems
are, by nature, more personal than ordinary haiku. Issho died
in the middle of winter, when snow had covered his prov-
ince. The "clouds in the west" *(nishi no kumo)* may be re-

garded as a seasonal image, but in this poem they probably refer to the messengers of Amida coming to greet the dead on their way to the Pure Land.

❖

ISSO

一　草

*Died on the seventeenth day of November, 1899
at the age of fifty-seven*

Cut your price!	*Makete oke*
What if I've gotten fifty-seven?	*gojūshichi de mo*
The year is nearly over!	*toshi no kure*

Isso takes his image from commerce. Fate sells life to man, and at the end of the years allotted to him, man must pay off the debt underwritten by fate at his birth. Isso, aware that he has already delayed payment for two years (as the life-span of man, according to one tradition, is fifty-five years), asks to defer payment for a little while longer, until the end of the year. He even requests a price cut, perhaps thinking of the practice of Japanese firms to hold clearance sales at the end of the year. But whether he gets such a discount or not, the poet seems to suggest that when he returns his life his situation will not be changed much anyway.

❖

JAKUA

寂　阿

Died on the fifth day of the fifth month, 1801

Cuckoo,
let's go—how bright
the western skies!

Hototogisu
iza ya akaruki
nishi no sora

The poet's pen name is composed of ideographs possessing religious significance. *Jaku* means tranquillity, death in a state of enlightenment; *a* is the first syllable in the name of Buddha Amida. From this we learn that Jakua was a Buddhist monk or priest.

❖

JAKURA

寂　羅

Died on the fifth day of June, 1906
at the age of fifty-nine

This year I want
to see the lotus
on the other side.

Mitaki kana
kotoshi no hasu wa
kano kishi ni

On the evening of Jakura's death, members of his family asked him to recite a death poem. He said the poem above and then tried to grasp a brush and write the words, but his strength did not hold out. He died, leaving a blank sheet of paper beside his bed.

In Buddhist literature, this world of life and death is called "this side" or "this shore," and nirvana, or enlightenment, is called "the other side" or "yonder shore." The passage from the world of illusion to the world of truth is likened to a boat trip from one side of a river to the other (compare the use of *higan,* p. 183).

❖

JIKKO

十 口

Died on the twenty-first day of the seventh month, 1791
at the age of sixty-nine

Family whispers	*Shinrui ga*
with the doctor—winter showers	*isha ni sasayaku*
pass through their sleeves.	*sode shigure*

When Japanese told secrets, they used to raise the sleeves of their robes to the sides of their faces. The whispering voices passing through the sleeves *(sode)* are likened to the sound of a gusty winter shower *(shigure).*

Jikko expressed his own opinion about death poems thus:

One evening a friend came to visit. We discussed haiku beside the stove and drank two or three cups of saké. We recalled the death poems of the old master poets, and tears streamed down our cheeks. We consoled ourselves, saying that even if the man dies, his death poem remains forever. For this reason there are men who prepare a death poem while still healthy. This may seem like exaggerated readiness, but fate plays tricks on us all, and we never know when it will ordain us to die. If death comes suddenly, we will have no time to say a word. It can therefore be understood why people prefer to write their death poem before their time. Some leave behind a distorted poem and claim there is no harm in that, because haiku poetry does not disdain popular speech. These people become the laughingstock of future generations. Great poets create outstanding death poems, and thus they show the strength of art, which fails not even in the hour of death. And so we continued well into the night. . . .

Jikko then "quotes" a death poem which he claims to have heard (it is likely that he wrote it himself). It is a poem in tanka form, and it reflects his opinion on death poetry:

Rather than leave behind me	*Waraigusa*
that which everyone will laugh at,	*nokosan yori mo*
I prepared my words beforehand.	*tsunezune ni*
Now, while dying,	*kyōji okitsure*
I'm at peace.	*ima wa ku mo nashi*[5]

It is interesting that the poem Jikko wrote before his death (the haiku above) does not, in fact, seem to have been prepared in advance. Perhaps because he had already paid due respect to tradition by preparing a poem beforehand, he was able, without difficulty, to compose this descriptive image of his last hours.

❖

JOMEI

丈　鳴

*Died on the seventh day of the ninth month, 1766
at the age of sixty-one*

Leaves of words:	*Koto no ha ya*
autumn colors	*ugokanu yama mo*
a still mountain.	*aki no iro*

There is a play on words here in the Japanese. The word *kotoba,* "language," is composed of *koto,* "word," and *ha,* "leaves." The poet, separating these two components into *koto no ha* creates the image of "leaves of words."

❖

JOSEKI

丈　石

*Died on the twenty-first day of the seventh month, 1779
at the age of eighty-five*

This must be	*Gokuraku ni*
my birthday there	*tanjōnichi wa*
in paradise.	*kyō nare ya*

❖

JOWA

常　和

Died on the second day of the second month, 1785
at the age of seventy-one

Second month:	*Kisaragi ya*
I wear a new bamboo hat	*atarashiki kasa*
and go home.	*kite kaeru*

This is not a death poem, but Jowa's last poem *(zekku),* a poem written before a poet's death without his having meant it as a death poem. It sometimes happened that a poet, though intending to write a death poem, died too suddenly to write one and left only a last poem. Some poets felt no need to follow the tradition of writing a death poem. Others wrote a death poem days, months, or even years before their death, so their last poem is not their death poem.

Jowa's case was of the first type. On the first day of the second month he stayed overnight with some relatives in his cottage and composed this poem in conversation there. The next day he died unexpectedly.

There is a play on words in the Japanese. *Kisaragi,* the old name of the second month, also means "dressed layer upon layer," thus suggesting the cold season. With this and the image of the bamboo hat, the poet evidently had in mind his return trip home from his cottage on a rainy and cold day.

❖

KAEN

可 焉

*Died on the thirteenth day of the ninth month, 1772
at the age of seventy-five*

A back-yard chrysanthemum	*Uragiku ya*
looked at the setting sun	*yūhi ni mukai*
and faded.	*shibominuru*

❖

KAFU

霞・夫

*Died on the twenty-ninth day of the ninth month, 1784
at the age of thirty-six*

If I must die	*Shinaba yo no*
then let me die before	*fuyu no konu ma to*
the winter comes.	*iiokeri*

Kafu was the son of a very wealthy family that dealt in Chinese medications. He neglected the family business, apparently because of his artistic and literary pursuits. The relatives got together, relieved him of his position in the family concern, and "housed him in a dwelling that they built for him." He seems to have spent the rest of his life as a monk.

Kafu was a friend of the artist and poet Buson, and like him he painted from time to time. Kafu died at the end of autumn, two days before the arrival of winter.

❖

KAFU

家 風

Died on the twenty-fourth day of the sixth month, 1827

Nights grow short:	*Mijikayo ya*
a dream of fifty years	*mihatenu yume no*
breaks off before it ends.	*gojū-nen*

Kafu was the son of Gazen (p. 167) and died a mere year and a half after his father. Sources do not give his age at the time of his death, but it can be inferred from "a dream of fifty years."

Mijikayo, "short night" refers to a night of summer. At such a time a person may sometimes waken from sleep with the feeling that the early dawn has interrupted his dream.

❖

KAGAI

花　街

Died on the seventh day of the fourth month, 1778

Barren branches: *Kare-eda ya*
the autumn left behind   *hakanaku nokoru*
a cicada's hollow cry.   *semi no koe*

❖

KAIGA

介　我

*Died on the sixteenth day of the sixth month, 1718
at the age of sixty-seven*

Strange—like messengers   *Omoshiro ya*
they fly left, fly right   *sau no tsukai no*
the fireflies.   *tobu hotaru*

Fireflies *(hotaru)*, whose lights flicker in the summer nights, seem to the poet like mysterious messengers that have come to carry away the souls of the dead.

❖

KAIKAI

父 々

Died in the sixth month, 1868
at the age of seventy-three

Round a flame	*Futatsu kite*
two tiger moths	*shi o arasou ya*
race to die.	*hitorimushi*

The tiger moth (*hitorimushi*, lit., fire-consuming insect) is a large and hairy moth with stripes. This insect is one of the images of summer, the season in which the poet died.

❖

KAISHO

快 笑

Died in 1914
at the age of seventy-two

Evening cherry-blossoms:	*Futokoro e*
I slip the inkstone back into my kimono	*suzuri shimau ya*
this one last time.	*yūzakura*

Suzuri is the inkstone on which an ink stick is rubbed to make the solution for brush painting. An inkstone has a specially made container for when it is not in use. It seems that

Kaisho knows that when he finishes this poem he will not write again, and that he will have no use for the inkstone that has served him so many years.

The word *futokoro* refers to the front of the kimono, where the two folds cross. It was used as a sort of pocket in which personal items could be carried.

❖

KANGA

喚 我

Died in 1812

A chill:	*Suzushiku mo*
my soul turns into	*tama wa gazō ni*
an icon.	*utsurikeri*

Gazo means "portrait" or "statue," perhaps of the Buddha, but not necessarily so. It is enough to see in the poem an image of the transition from a world of heat and movement to cold immobility.

❖

KANGYU

閑 牛

Died in 1861

It is indeed like that—
and I had never noticed
dew on grass.

Kakuzo tomo
kokoro no tsukazu
kusa no tsuyu

❖

KANNA

冠 那

Died on the fifteenth day of the seventh month, 1744

Autumn breeze:
driftwood
landing lightly on the bank.

Nagaregi no
yoru kata yasashi
aki no kaze

❖

KANSHU

竿 秋

Died on the eleventh day of the ninth month, 1772
at the age of seventy-eight

Although the autumn moon
has set, its light
lingers on my chest.

Meigetsu no
ato ni mo mune no
hikari kana

Meigetsu is the full moon on the ides of the eighth lunar month
(about mid-October by the solar calendar). On that night the

Japanese sit out to view the moon in the clear skies of autumn.

Various customs are attached to the appearance of the full autumn moon: offerings of fruit and flowers, preparing food especially for the occasion, burning incense, and writing poetry about the moon's beauty.

❖

KARAI

化　来

Died on the twenty-eighth day of the ninth month, 1778
at the age of fifty-seven

Why should I hesitate?	*Mayoyasenu*
I have a travel permit	*tōri kitte no*
from Amida Buddha.	*Namu Amida*

Unlike death poems in which allusions to Buddhism express comfort in the next world, this poem juxtaposes "travel permit" *(tori kitte)* and Amida Buddha, with a trace of irony.

❖

KARI

花　里

Died on the twelfth day of the third month, 1770
at the age of sixty-seven

How sad: cherry blossoms   *Ushi ya hana*
turn to clouds that   *ware o mukaeru*
come to greet me.   *kumo to nari*

Many Japanese poets have likened the splendid sight of cherry blossoms to clouds of flowers. Kari died in the spring during the cherry-blossom season, and it seems that he felt sorrow while viewing them for the last time.

According to Buddhist tradition, clouds appear in the western sky at the hour of one's death to escort one to the other world.

❖

KASEI

歌 成

Died on the second day of the second month, 1859
at the age of sixty-two

The ash I leave behind   *Hai ni naru*
is just a moxa treatment   *nagori mo kyū no*
on the second of the month. *futsuka kana*

Moxa treatment *(kyu)* is an ancient Oriental healing art in which a substance from leaves of the wormwood is burned on certain parts of the body. The burning is said to stimulate the nervous system, cleanse the blood, ease pain, and heal various diseases. Kasei likens the ashes that will remain after his cremation to the small burned spot left by cauterization. Moxa treatment may bring relief from ailments of the body, but the burning of the body after death eliminates the source of all ailments. The poem was written the very day the poet died.

Kasei was a Kabuki artist whose theater name was Otozo.

❖

KASENJO

歌 川 女

Died on the twenty-sixth day of the seventh month, 1776
at the age of sixty-two

Depths of cold	*Okusoko no*
unfathomable	*shirenu samusa ya*
ocean roar.	*umi no oto*

Kasenjo was a geisha in a resort area of mineral springs. At an older age, she shaved her head and became a Buddhist nun. It is noteworthy that the "cold" *(samusa)* of her poem does not seem to be the "cold" used in haiku poetry to designate the season, but the cold of death.

❖

KASENNI

花 千 尼

Died on the twenty-seventh day of the seventh month, 1729

Cicada of the night	*Yoru no semi*
one autumn moon	*aki hito-tsuki ya*
Sumida River.	*Sumida-gawa*

If we compute the date of Kasenni's death by the Gregorian calendar, we find that she died one month after the beginning of autumn.

The Sumida River flows through the eastern part of Tokyo into Tokyo Bay.

❖

KASSAN

葛 三

Died on the twelfth day of the sixth month, 1818
at the age of fifty-seven

Summer	*Mi no ue no*
is upon me:	*natsu ya hasu no*
a lotus leaf.	*ichimai-ba*

❖

KATO

可 斗

Died on the ninth day of September, 1908
at the age of sixty-one

The moon departs:	*Asagao ya*
frost falls upon the	*tsuki no wakare o*
morning glory.	*hana no hie*

❖

KEIDO

径 童

Died in about 1750
past the age of thirty

The cuckoo's voice	*Shinuru hi wa*
is all the more intriguing	*nao omoshiroshi*
as I die.	*kankodori*

Among the little to be found about Keido in old sources, it is perhaps worth mentioning that he was a hermit monk who lived in the mountains.

The *kankodori* is a kind of cuckoo, similar in appearance and habits to the *hototogisu* (see p. 142).

❖

KEIDO

径 童

Died on the seventh day of the fourth month, 1787
at the age of seventy-three

Bound homeward under	*Kokyō e no*
clear summer skies:	*hare ya uzuki no*
bird feathers, flowers.	*hana torige*

Uzuki, the fourth month of the lunar calendar (corresponding
approximately to the end of May and the beginning of June),
is the first month of summer.

❖

KEIZAN

慶 山

Died on the twenty-fourth day of the eighth month, 1750
at the age of forty-four

Border of the realm,	*Kunizakai*
bound by cane on both sides—	*sayū no tsue ya*
moon above the bamboo.	*tsuki no take*

The "border" *(kunizakai),* evidently the frontier between
the worlds of the living and the dead, refers perhaps to the
mountains crossed by the dead to reach the other world.

The view of the moon above the bamboo grove may be a glimpse of the no-man's-land on the frontier of the two worlds.

The bamboo *(take)* is a perennial plant, the largest in the grass family. Its stems are large and strong, often resembling tree trunks.

❖

KENJU

乾 十

Died on the twenty-seventh day of the second month, 1759
at the age of eighty

The melting snows:	*Yukidoke ya*
an edifice	*hachijū-nen no*
of eighty years.	*tsukurimono*

The sources say that Kenju owned and managed a brothel in the red-light district of Edo. The word *tsukurimono* is used for anything which does not come about naturally, but is produced or shaped by the human mind. My eighty years, Kenju seems to be telling us, are but a contrivance which melts like a snowman when the spring comes.

❖

KIBA

鬼 馬

Died in 1868
at the age of ninety

My old body:	*Oi no mi ya*
a drop of dew grown	*hazue no omoru*
heavy at the leaf tip.	*tsuyu no tama*

❖

KIBAI

其 梅

Died on the twelfth day of the second month, 1788
at the age of seventy

My one wish	*Negawaku wa*
is to live in the capital	*mui no miyako o*
of non-action.	*sumidokoro*

Mui is the Japanese pronunciation of the Chinese *wu wei,*
the Taoist philosophy of "non-action" (see p. 68). The term
also appears in certain Buddhist writings as a synonym for
nirvana, but in Zen Buddhist writings, the meaning of the
word more closely approaches that of the Taoists.

❖

KIFU

起 風

Died in autumn, 1898

Cutting a swath	*Tsuyu fukaki*
through thick-dewed grass,	*kusa fumiwakete*
I set out.	*kadode kana*

The exact date of Kifu's death is unknown, but he is said to have died in the autumn, the season of dew.

❖

KIGEN

其 諺

Died on the twenty-third day of the eighth month, 1736
at the age of seventy-one

Seventy-one!	*Nanajūichi*
How did	*yō wa motsutaru*
a dewdrop last?	*tsuyu no tama*

❖

KIKO

其 香

Died on the second day of the fifth month, 1823
at the age of fifty-two

That which blossoms	*Sakeba chiru*
falls, the way of all flesh	*mi no yukusue ya*
in this world of flowers.	*hana sekai*

❖

KIMPO

芹 甫

Died on the third day of September, 1894

Today is the day	*Miosame no*
for one last view	*kyō to wa narinu*
of Mount Fuji.	*Fuji-no-yama*

The volcanic Mount Fuji, whose snow-capped peak is visible from Tokyo on clear days, is one of the world's most beautiful mountains. A holy mountain in Japanese tradition, it has given rise to many legends. Mount Fuji has appeared and reappeared in painting and poetry as a symbol of the sublime beauty for which the soul of man yearns.

❖

KIMPU

琴 風

*Died on the seventh day of the second month, 1726
at the age of sixty*

One gulp,	*Hito-iki ni*
a taste of nectar!	*kono ajiwai zo*
Water in the spring.	*haru no mizu*

With the winter runoff and spring rains, the banks of lakes and rivers overflow. Plants begin to bud, and the water swarms with fish. "Water in the [season of] spring" *(haru no mizu)* is a seasonal image in haiku, yet it hints as well at *shinimizu,* the water given to dying persons.

❖

KIN'EI

金 映

*Died on the sixteenth day of the eighth month, 1778
at the age of forty-five*

The autumn flowers	*Gokuraku no*
of my prayer bear	*tane zo kusabana*
seeds of paradise.	*Namu Amida*

Kin'ei died in autumn, when grasses blossom. He carries his prayer like he would a flowering plant, and when the petals fall and the seeds are released, he will be, so he hopes, "replanted" in paradise.

❖

KINKO

錦 江

*Died on the twenty-seventh day of the seventh month, 1860
at the age of sixty*

Within the vast and empty
autumn night
dawn breaks.

*Aki no yo mo
tada kūjaku to
akete yuku*

❖

KIN'U

琴 雨

*Died on the second day of the third month, 1817
at the age of sixty-two*

How leisurely the cherry
blossoms bloom this year, unhurried
by their doom.

*Yururi saku
kotoshi no hana no
kakugo kana*

Kin'u died in spring, together with the cherry blossoms of
the year. *Kakugo* signifies courageous resignation to fate.

❖

KISEI

亀 世

Died on the eighteenth day of the ninth month, 1764
at the age of seventy-seven

Ninth-month moon:	*Nembutsu mo*
of late, when I have said	*makoto ni narinu*
my prayer, I've meant it.	*nochi no tsuki*

*   *   *   *

Since I was born	*Umarete wa*
I have to die,	*shinuru hazu nari*
and so . . .	*sore naraba*

Both of these haiku appear as Kisei's death poems in old
sources. Kisei died five days after *nochi no tsuki* (lit., later
moon), the second of two holidays celebrating the autumn
moon. *Nembutsu* refers to the prayer *Namu Amida Butsu.*

❖

KIYU

亀 祐

Died in about 1820

Evening:	*Chichi haha no*
I, too, the dew of those who bred me,	*wagō no tsuyu mo*
am twilit.	*kyō no kure*

This death poem was inscribed on Kiyu's gravestone. Kiyu was a potter, and it is said that even his tombstone was made of clay.

Dew, a symbol of transience and also a season word signifying autumn, in this poem has further connotations of sexuality and fertility. A poet's reference to himself as the product of his parents' union is rare in haiku.

❖

KIZAN

葵　山

Died on the fifteenth day of the eighth month, 1786

Clouds drifting off:	*Ukigumo no*
the sight of	*harete jōdo no*
moonlit heavens.	*tsukimi kana*

Ukigumo means "floating clouds," an image often used in Japanese literature to represent the life of man. *Jodo* is the Pure Land in the West.

On the evening of the fifteenth day of the eighth lunar month, the Japanese go outdoors to celebrate the sight of the full autumn moon, a custom known as *tsukimi*, "moon viewing." Haiku poets take up their brushes to describe the beauty of the moon in verse.

❖

KIZAN

箕　山

*Died on the fourth day of the twelfth month, 1851
at the age of sixty-four*

When I am gone   *Rusu naredo*
will someone care for   *tou hito mo kana*
the chrysanthemum I leave?   *nokorigiku*

Nokorigiku, "remaining chrysanthemum," appears here with
a twofold meaning: a chrysanthemum still in bloom at the
end of autumn, when most of the others have withered, and
a chrysanthemum which remains after the owner of the gar-
den has died.

❖

KOHA

香　波

Died on the fourteenth day of August, 1897

I cast the brush aside—   *Fude nagete*
from here on I'll speak to the moon   *tsuki ni mono iu*
face to face.   *bakari nari*

❖

KOJU

湖 十

Died on the twenty-fourth day of the seventh month, 1806

And if I do
become a spirit—
the party's over.

*Shōryō ni
ato no matsuri to
narinikeri*

Koju died some time after the end of the Bon Festival and thus spoiled his chance to return to his home as a spirit.

Ato no matsuri, literally, "after the festival," is an idiomatic expression meaning "to miss one's chance," "to come too late." In this poem, the expression can thus be understood literally—"after the celebration of the Bon Festival"—or in the wider sense that the poet has no more hope to live.

❖

KONKAN

昆 寛

*Died on the twenty-eighth day of the ninth month, 1801
at the age of fifty-eight*

When I leave the world
on my way back I'll carry
just one beggar's bag.

*Yo o sareba
zuda hitotsu nari
modoru tabi*

This stone made ready for my tomb is but a passing shower in my heart.	*Tsukurioku* *haka mo kokoro no* *shigure kana*

These two poems are engraved on the poet's tombstone. *Zuda* is a short form of *zudabukuro*, a sack strapped on by Zen monks as they go from door to door begging food.

❖

KORAKU

古 楽

Died on the eleventh day of the fifth month, 1837
at the age of fifty-seven

The joy of dewdrops in the grass as they turn back to vapor.	*Moto no mizu ni* *kaeru zo ureshi* *kusa no tsuyu*

❖

KOSAI

コ 斎

Died on the twenty-first day of the seventh month, 1688

Poor Kosai—   *Aware nari*
but one lantern   *tōro hitotsu ni*
to his name.   *nushi Kosai*

The *toro* is a lantern with a candle in it, lit during the Bon
Festival in memory of those who have died.

Kosai was apparently a friend of Kikaku's, as the latter
wrote the following poem immediately after Kosai's death:

Autumn ends: *Sono hito no*
he didn't leave behind   *ibiki sae nashi*
even a snore.   *aki no kure*[6]

On the third anniversary of Kosai's death, a poet named
Kifu composed this poem:

Three years: *Mitose haya*
even the lantern   *tōro hitotsu mo*
is no more.   *nakarikeri*[7]

❖

KOSEKI

敲 石

Died in the seventh month, 1788

Swear to me, pine,   *Chigirioku*
for many years   *matsu ya iku-tose*
to keep on young and green.   *waka midori*

❖

KOSON

孤　村

Died on the thirty-first day of August, 1920
at the age of thirty-eight

I die	*Fuyō saku*
the evening of the day	*hi yūbe ni*
the hibiscus blooms.	*shinuru kana*

The *fuyo,* a garden plant originating in China and found in the warmer regions of Japan, is a species of hibiscus. At the beginning of autumn it blooms in pink, scarlet, and white; its petals wither in the course of a single day.

This poem contains only fifteen syllables in the original. It is likely that two syllables were left out during printing.

❖

KOYO

紅　葉

Died on the thirtieth day of October, 1903
at the age of thirty-seven

If I must die	*Shinaba aki*
let it be autumn	*tsuyu no hinuma zo*
ere the dew is dry.	*omoshiroki*

Ozaki Koyo was a major novelist of the Meiji period. Influenced by the writings of Ihara Saikaku (p. 274), Koyo's works are on romantic themes. Koyo suffered from stomach cancer during the last several years of his life and died in his home.

❖

KOZAN

皷 山

Died on the twenty-sixth day of the ninth month, 1747
at the age of forty-six

How sublime—	*Arigata ya*
a boat beneath the moon	*tsuki no funauta*
and from within, a prayer.	*Namu Amida*

A *funauta,* "boat song," is a song sung by sailors or by boat passengers sailing by moonlight. Such a song is not a prayer, of course, but it sounds to the dying poet like the chant *Namu Amida Butsu.*

❖

KUSAMARU

草 丸

Died in 1836
at the age of fifty-two

My morning porridge,	*Asagayu no*
and then I'll go to see	*za kara mi ni iku*
the willow blossom.	*yanagi kana*

❖

KYOHAKU

虚 白

Died on the last day of the tenth month, 1847
at the age of seventy-five

I am not worthy	*Ōkenaki*
of this crimson carpet:	*toko no nishiki ya*
autumn maple leaves.	*chiri-momiji*

Momiji is a general term for the sight of leaves in autumn, but it refers principally to the color of maple leaves. The leaves of this tree turn deep red at the end of autumn, making the forests covering the mountains look as if they have caught fire.

Already in ancient Japanese poetry, the sight of maple leaves is likened to a silk carpet *(toko no nishiki)*. Kyohaku died at a time when the autumn leaves were laid out like a red carpet to the other world.

❖

KYOKUSAI

曲 斎

Died on the twenty-ninth day of July, 1874
at the age of fifty-eight

When you contemplate the waters	*Akatsuki ya*
at day break, you can hear	*mizu kanzureba*
the lotus blossom.	*hasu no oto*

It is widely held in Japan that the lotus makes a noise when it opens, but there is no scientific basis for this belief. It arose as part of the Buddhist tradition that sees in the lotus the flower of paradise.

❖

KYO'ON

去 音

Died on the tenth day of the eleventh month, 1749
at the age of sixty-three

A last fart:	*Yume no ha ka*
are these the leaves	*chiru sharakusashi*
of my dream, vainly falling?	*saigo no he*

In the original, the image of a dream is combined with the cruder image of passing wind. The transition from one to the other is made by a play on words: *sharakusashi* means "boastfulness" or "vanity"; the latter part of the word alone, *kusashi,* means "stench."

❖

KYOSHU

虚　舟

Died on the sixteenth day of the sixth month, 1769
at the age of eighty

A journey of no return:	*Sokonuke ya*
the wanderer's sack is	*kaeranu tabi no*
bottomless.	*zudabukuro*

Kyoshu prefaces his death poem with a phrase from Zen Buddhist writings: "I came from nowhere and go nowhere." The image of a bottomless sack, which also fits the spirit of Zen, indicates that the wanderer's consciousness is freed from concepts like "life" and "death."

❖

KYUTARO

久　太　郎

Died on the twentieth day of February, 1928
at the age of thirty-six

Tender winds above the snow	*Moromoro no*
melt many kinds	*nayami mo kiyuru*
of suffering.	*yuki no kaze*

Kyutaro started working as a messenger boy for a commercial firm at the age of twelve. A year later, on Emperor's Day (February 11) he went out to play in the snow. The head clerk considered such behavior an affront to the nation and scolded him. The thirteen-year-old Kyutaro wrote this poem:

In heavy snow	*Ōyuki de*
I clean forgot	*kokki dasu no mo*
to raise the nation's flag.	*wasurekeri*

In later years Kyutaro lived among workers and day laborers in Tokyo and became a radical anarchist. In 1923 he fired a gun at a government official and was sentenced to life imprisonment. He committed suicide in his cell, leaving his death poem behind him.

❖

MABUTSU

馬 仏

Died on the twenty-first day of the twelfth month, 1696

The snowman's eyes	*Me wa yoko ni*
are on the level; his nose	*hana wa tate nari*
stands straight.	*yukibotoke*

The snowman in this poem is not only a seasonal image, but also a symbol of transience.

Phrases such as "the eyes lie horizontally, the nose vertically" (given an alternate wording in the translation) and "the threshold is horizontal and vertical the pillar" appear in Zen writings as an expression of an enlightened point of view. Such remarks do not proceed from the understanding of any so-called truth, but from the reflection of the world in the consciousness that, like a clear mirror, has nothing in itself and neither adds to nor takes away from the thing it reflects.

❖

MABUTSU

馬 仏

*Died on the fifteenth day of the eighth month, 1874
at the age of seventy-nine*

Moon in a barrel:	*Itsu nukeru*
you never know just when	*soko tomo shirazu*
the bottom will fall out.	*oke no tsuki*

Mabutsu died on the day of the full autumn moon. (The date of his death is evidently given in the old system).

❖

MASAHIDE

正 秀

*Died on the third day of the eighth month, 1723
at the age of sixty-seven*

While I walk on	*Yuku toki wa*
the moon keeps pace beside me:	*tsuki ni narabite*
friend in the water.	*mizu no tomo*

Masahide, a doctor by profession, lived most of his life in the town of Zeze on Lake Biwa. He studied haiku under Basho, whom he very much admired. Around 1688 Masahide's storehouse burned down, and he wrote the following poem, which was much praised by Basho.

Now that my storehouse	*Kura yakete*
has burned down, nothing	*sawaru mono naki*
conceals the moon.	*tsukimi kana*

It seems that Masahide became very poor after his storehouse burned down. His poet friend Jozen, who came to visit him in 1703, reported that Masahide had no blanket for his two children, and had to cover them with mosquito netting.

❖

MASUMI KATO

十寸見 河東

Died on the twentieth day of the seventh month, 1725
at the age of forty-two

I draw the willow
branch down low
below my hips.

Hikiyosete
koshi yori shita no
yanagi kana

Masumi Kato was the founder of a family of ballad *(joruri)* writers. He originated his own style of narrative, which came to be called Kato-bushi.

❖

MASUMI KATO

十寸見 河東

Died on the twenty-first day of the first month, 1796
at the age of seventy

The path to paradise
is paved with bright
plum petals.

Gokuraku no
michi mo akarushi
ume sakura

This Masumi Kato was the sixth head of the family of ballad writers founded by the Masumi Kato above. This haiku appears on the poet's gravestone.

The path "paved with bright plum petals" is the way to paradise. If we note, however, that Kato's death did indeed take place during the plum-blossom season, we can understand that this world and the next are not really so far from one another.

❖

MASUMI KATO

十寸見 河東

Died on the twenty-fourth day of the second month, 1825
at the age of sixty-four

The surface	*Samazama na*
of the water mirrors	*kage mo utsurishi*
many things.	*mizu no aya*

This Masumi Kato represents the seventh generation of the family of Kato-bushi writers. He succeeded the Masumi Kato whose poem appears above.

❖

MEISETSU

鳴 雪

Died on the twentieth day of February, 1926
at the age of eighty

My only hope against
the cold—
one hot-water bottle.

Tada tanomu
tōba hitotsu no
samusa kana

This is Meisetsu's last poem. A *toba* is a hot-water bottle used for warming the feet in winter, but there may be a pun on this word in that, when written with different characters, it refers to the long wooden tablet bearing a Buddhist prayer placed at one's grave. Relatives and close friends buy such prayer tablets, so the deceased may have several written for him. A single tablet (as the poem would read if this *toba* were used) would thus imply loneliness or friendlessness.

❖

MICHIKAZE

三 千 風

Died on the fourth day of the fourth month, 1709
at the age of sixty-nine

Today I put on summer
clothes and journey
to a world I haven't seen yet.

Kyō zo haya
minu yo no tabi e
koromogae

Michikaze is described by his contemporaries as a man greedy for wealth and fame, and his name was linked with geisha of Edo, Kyoto, and Osaka. Late in life he "repented" and wrote a tanka mocking himself for his former way of life and denouncing the vanity in his pursuit of fame.

Koromogae is the change from heavy winter clothing to lighter summer robes, done in the first part of the fourth month by the old calendar (about the middle of May). The use of this term in Michikaze's death poem gives evidence that his date of death, about which various sources are in conflict, is correct as stated here.

❖

MINTEISENGAN

眠亭賤丸

*Died on the fifth day of the fourth month, 1844
at the age of sixty-seven*

Fall, plum petals,	*Ka no aru o*
fall—and leave behind the memory	*omoide ni shite*
of scent.	*koboreume*

❖

MITOKU

未　得

*Died on the eighteenth day of the seventh month, 1669
at the age of eighty-two*

The foam on the last water	*Mune suzushi*
has dissolved	*kie o matsugo no*
my mind is clear.	*mizu no awa*

The death of Mitoku, who was a money changer in Edo, is recounted by his son Mitaku:

> Mitoku took ill in the first part of the fifth month. On the twenty-ninth day of the following month his breathing ceased, but it began again after water was splashed on his face. When I said to him, "You must be suffering terribly," he did not answer directly, saying only, "Bring me the inkstone." After dipping his brush in ink he wrote his death poem . . . and handed it to me. After this it looked as though he lost consciousness. On the eighteenth day of the seventh month he died, murmuring the name of Buddha.[8]

Matsugo no mizu, "water of the last moments," like *shini-mizu,* refers to the water used to moisten the lips of the dying.

The poem contains a play on words. *Matsu* in *matsugo no mizu* means "the end," but *matsu* also means "to wait." The phrase *kie o matsu* can thus be read, "I await my dissolution."

❖

MOKUDO

木　導

*Died on the twenty-second day of the sixth month, 1723
at the age of fifty-eight*

l constantly aspire
to be the first to pierce
my dagger in the eggplant.

*Ki ni kakaru
ichiban yari no
nasubi kana*

Mokudo apparently tries, with the strange image of piercing a dagger into an eggplant *(nasubi)*, to blend the fighting spirit (he belonged to the samurai class) with the spirit of haiku. The eggplant is a seasonal image for summer, during which the poet died; with a dagger stuck into it, the eggplant symbolizes the enemy's head.

We are unfortunately not entitled to hope that the poem was written in jest, for the warrior-poet prefaces it with an explanation:

> In times of war the samurai were the first to stab their daggers into their enemies. We are familiar with many stories about these bold warriors. Today peace reigns in the world and warriors no longer go forth into battle. They continue, however, with military exercises, so that in time of need they will be ready to fight zealously, till word of their courage echoes throughout Japan and the entire world.[9]

❖

MOMEN

木 綿

Died on the twenty-ninth day of the fifth month, 1788

Clouds breaking up,	*Kumo harete*
and lo—true skies:	*makoto no sora ya*
the voice of a cicada.	*semi no koe*

❖

MORITAKE

守 武

Died on the eighth day of the eighth month, 1549
at the age of seventy-seven

Today	*Asagao ni*
my life is mirrored in	*kyō wa miyuran*
a morning glory.	*wagayo kana*

Moritake, a Shinto priest at the large shrine of Ise, was skilled in writing *renga*. The refined humor of his style influenced haiku poetry by turning it from games of wit to literature in its own right.

There exists another version of Moritake's death poem. The poet Kikaku writes:

Kakei, a pupil of Basho's, edited a collection of poems called *Aranoshu* and included in it a death poem ostensibly written by Moritake: "Twilight / a eulogy for petals / falling [*Chiru hana o / Namu Amida Butsu to / yūbe kana*]." I am convinced that this is a mistake, for a Shinto priest is not likely to abandon the world with [a Buddhist prayer]. It is more likely that Moritake merely wrote the poem after seeing flowers wilt.[10]

❖

NAKAMICHI

仲 道

Died on the second day of January, 1893

At the crossroad of my life and death a cuckoo cries.	*Ikishini no* *oiwakezaka ya* *hototogisu*
Ice in a hot world: my life melts.	*Atsui yo ni* *kōri to kiyuru* *inochi kana*

❖

NAMAGUSAI TAZUKURI

腥 斎 佃

Died on the sixteenth day of the eighth month, 1858
at the age of seventy-two

In fall the willow tree recalls its bygone glory.	*Aisareshi* *ga o omoide ni* *chiru yanagi*

Namagusai Tazukuri, whose name means literally "peasant reeking of fish," was born to a poor fishmonger. His parents died when he was young, and he was adopted by a fisherman. Namagusai Tazukuri was the fifth head of the *senryu* school.

❖

NANDAI

南 台

*Died on the twenty-fourth day of the twelfth month, 1817
at the age of thirty-one*

Since time began	*Kanete naki*
the dead alone know peace.	*mi koso yasukere*
Life is but melting snow.	*yuki no michi*

❖

OKANO KIN'EMON KANEHIDE

岡野金右衛門包秀

*Died on the fourth day of the second month, 1703
at the age of twenty-four*

Over the fields of	*Sono nioi*
last night's snow—	*yuki no ashita no*
plum fragrance.	*noume kana*

Okano Kin'emon Kanehide was one of the forty-seven samurai who participated in one of the most exciting incidents in Japanese history. In 1701, a feudal lord named Asano Nagamori was ordered to hold a reception in honor of the

emperor's messenger. A high official by the name of Kira Yo-
shinaka, who was appointed by the shogun to be in charge
of ceremony, was to instruct Asano in ceremonial etiquette.
Kira treated Asano with contempt. Asano, his pride wounded,
drew his sword and struck Kira. Since the incident took place
in the castle at Edo, in the grounds of which the drawing of
weapons was strictly forbidden, Asano was ordered to take
his own life by *seppuku* on that very day. He did so. Asano's
estate was confiscated by the government, and the shogun
rejected the petition brought to him by Asano's retainers to
hand over the estate to the younger brother of the deceased.

Thus Asano's warriors became *ronin,* samurai without a
lord. Forty-seven of them swore to avenge their master by
killing Kira. To keep from attracting attention to themselves,
they scattered to different parts of the country and waited for
the proper moment. It came two years later, when Kira began
to relax the security measures he had taken to protect him-
self. On a snowy morning of the second month, 1702, the
samurai broke into Kira's mansion and killed him. They then
turned themselves over to the government.

In taking their revenge, the forty-seven samurai acted in
accordance with the moral code that forbade them to "live
under the same sky as the enemy of their lord." They gained
sympathy in many circles of society, and the shogun himself
was inclined to pardon them. In the end, however, those
who insisted on enforcing the law prevailed, and a year after
the incident took place, all forty-seven warriors were ordered
to kill themselves by *seppuku.* This event excited the imagina-
tion of the Japanese, and the forty-seven samurai gained an
immortal place in the history and the literature of their
country.

❖

OKYO

鴬 居

Died on the twenty-fifth day of August, 1890
at the age of eighty-three

This phantasm	*Chiru to mishi*
of falling petals vanishes into	*maboroshi kiete*
moon and flowers . . .	*hana ni tsuki*

Hana, referring to cherry blossoms, is a season word for spring, whereas *tsuki* usually refers to the full moon of autumn. Through his death poem, Okyo transcends the illusions of this world of changing elements and seasons to a world where a never-setting moon lights everlasting flowers.

❖

ONITSURA

鬼 貫

Died on the second day of the eighth month, 1738
at the age of seventy-eight

Give my dream back,	*Yume kaese*
raven! The moon you woke me to	*karasu no samasu*
is misted over.	*kiri no tsuki*

Kiri (mist) generally appears in haiku poetry as an autumnal image. What was the dream cut off by the raven's cry? Did the poet see a vision of the full moon floating in clear skies?

❖

OSEN

横 船

Died on the fifteenth day of the ninth month, 1696
at the age of forty-four

What a lark!	*Omoshiro ya*
Swinging my arms I set off:	*te futte mairu*
a winter rainstorm.	*murashigure*

Murashigure is a sudden winter rainstorm accompanied by wind. It falls for the most part in mountainous areas, stopping as quickly as it starts.

In the Japanese, the word *mairu* may refer either to the poet's departure, or to the coming rainstorm in the last line. It is preferable, however, to think in terms of the former interpretation—Osen walking off amusing himself with the thought that he, too, came and went through the world with the suddenness of a rainstorm.

❖

OTO

鶯　塘

Died on the thirty-first day of May, 1935
at the age of sixty-five

At night my sleep	*Natsu kage o*
embraces the summer shadows	*inochi to daite*
of my life.	*neru yo kana*

❖

OTSUCHI

乙　池

Died on the twenty-ninth day of the tenth month, 1872
at the age of sixty-four

O white chrysanthemum—	*Shiragiku ya*
man, too,	*hito no sakari mo*
passes his prime.	*hodo ga aru*

Otsuchi died when chrysanthemum flowers succumb to late autumn frost.

❖

OTSUIN

乙 因

Died on the twenty-fifth day of the fourth month, 1807

Hidden among the roots	*Kusa no ne ni*
of grass I hear	*kakurete kikan*
a cuckoo.	*kankodori*

Otsuin died in early June, when cuckoos migrate from southern Asia to Japan, their voices filling the air and evoking nostalgia in those who hear them.

The phrase "hidden among the roots / of grass" may be an allusion to the state after death. Although most Japanese no longer bury their dead, but cremate them, the idea of burial underground persists as a literary image.

❖

OZUI

応 随

Died on the tenth day of the first month, 1783
at the age of fifty-two

Still tied to the world,	*Yo no hazuna*
I cool off and lose	*hiekiru ware mo*
my form.	*katachi nashi*

The phrase *yo no hazuna* means "halter of this world" and refers, apparently, to the body that ties one to this life.

❖

RA-IN

羅　院

Died on the thirteenth day of the tenth month, 1779
at the age of thirty-six

My body in its autumn:	*Mi no aki zo*
a ragbag as rough	*hechima no kawa no*
as gourdskin.	*dambukuro*

Ra-in's father (also called Ra-in) died less than three months before his son, on the twenty-ninth day of the seventh month, at the age of seventy-one. The father's death poem also opens with the words "my body in its autumn." He did indeed die in autumn, but his son, who died in winter, apparently preferred to honor his father rather than preserve haiku tradition.

Hechima is the Japanese word for the loofah, a climbing vine with gourd-like fruit first brought to Japan from China in the seventeenth century. The Japanese use the plant for various purposes: when dried, its fibers become a scrubbing brush; in autumn, the stalk is cut about a half meter from the ground, and the sap which runs out is used by women as skin lotion; the sap is also taken as a cough remedy.

❖

RAIRAI

来 々

*Died on the seventeenth day of the ninth month, 1780
at the age of fifty-four*

I take leave	*Katabira wa*
of autumn dressed in a	*ware ga aki saru*
summer shroud.	*koromo kana*

Katabira means "robe of hemp." In Buddhist burial cere-
monies, the dead are wrapped in a shroud made of hemp.
Since summer robes are also made of this material, the last
two lines of the poem can be read, ". . . dressed in / summer
clothes." Rairai died in late autumn.

❖

RAISHI

来 之

Died on the twenty-seventh day of the ninth month, 1795

You've done your duty	*Kyō made wa*
till today,	*yo ni tsutometaru*
old scarecrow.	*kakashi kana*

The scarecrow *(kakashi)* appears in haiku poetry as a season word for autumn, when the rice is harvested.

❖

RAIZAN

来 山

*Died on the third day of the tenth month, 1716
at the age of sixty-three*

Farewell, sire—	*Suwa saraba*
like snow, from water come	*mizu yori mizu e*
to water gone.	*yuki no michi*

Raizan, a contemporary of Basho's, learned to write haiku at the age of eight and was authorized to teach and criticize haiku at the age of eighteen. It was said of Raizan that he never put his wine glass down and that he never stayed sober for so much as a day at a time. Rumor had it that he loved a doll rather than a woman and for that reason did not get married. In fact, he was married twice.

Just before his death, Raizan wrote a humorous death poem in tanka form:

Raizan has died	*Raizan wa*
to pay for the mistake	*umareta toga de*
of being born:	*shinuru nari*
for this he blames no one,	*sore de urami mo*
and bears no grudge.	*nanimo kamo nashi*

❖

RANDO

鸞　動

Died on the thirtieth day of the seventh month, 1686
at the age of twenty-two

For a moment there   *Ne wa tokiwa*
the ivy dyed   *shibashi momijinu*
the evergreen trunk red.   *matsu no tsuta*

The *tsuta* is a clinging vine found throughout Japan, climbing on stones and trees and covering fences and walls. In autumn its leaves turn red before falling. The evergreen mentioned in the poem is the pine *(matsu)*.

❖

RANGAI

嵐　外

Died on the twenty-sixth day of the third month, 1845
at the age of seventy-five

I wish to die   *Fuji-no-yama*
a sudden death with eyes   *minagara shitaki*
fixed on Mount Fuji.   *tonshi kana*

❖

RANSEKI

蘭 石

*Died on the second day of the seventh month, 1738
at the age of fifty-five*

This last night of nights
bush clover whispers
"Buddha, Buddha . . ."

*Hagi no koe
Mida to kiku yo o
kagiri kana*

Mida is short for Amida, the Buddha who rules the Pure Land in the West.

❖

RANSEKI

蘭 石

*Died on the twelfth day of the first month, 1782
at the age of sixty-nine*

Each day the absent grow
more numerous—tree branches
frozen.

*Naki wa kazu
sō hi to natte
eda samushi*

This Ranseki is the son of the preceding Ranseki.

❖

RANSETSU

嵐 雪

Died on the thirteenth day of the tenth month, 1707
at the age of fifty-four

One leaf lets go, and	*Hito-ha chiru*
then another takes	*totsu hito-ha chiru*
the wind.	*kaze no ue*

Ransetsu was a pupil of Basho's. Basho praised Ransetsu's poetry, but the poet Kyoriku said it was "anemic," and compared it to someone "who invites guests to a feast and serves no more than a menu."

Old sources say that Ransetsu's first wife was a bathing-house prostitute. She died after giving birth to a son, where-upon Ransetsu took a geisha as his wife. The couple became converts to Zen Buddhism. It is further stated that during a certain period, Ransetsu lived in the poet Kikaku's house, and that "he had not even a mat to lie on."

The word *totsu* is a cry of challenge uttered by Zen monks upon enlightenment. Another possible translation is "A leaf falls, ho! / Another leaf falls / high on the wind."

❖

REKISEN

礫 川

Died after 1834
past the age of eighty-six

Let them bloom or	*Saku mo yoshi*
let them die—it's all the same:	*chiru mo Yoshino no*
cherry trees on Mount Yoshino.	*yamazakura*

Mount Yoshino, near the city of Nara, is famed for its beauty during the cherry-blossom season.

❖

RENSEKI

練 石

Died on the fifth day of the seventh month, 1789
at the age of eighty-eight

I cleansed the mirror	*Harai arai*
of my heart—now it reflects	*kokoro no tsuki no*
the moon.	*kagami kana*

❖

RETSUZAN

列 山

Died on the twenty-fifth day of the eighth month, 1826
at the age of thirty-seven

The night I understood	*Tsuyu no yo to*
this is a world of dew,	*satoru sono yo o*
I woke up from my sleep.	*nezame kana*

❖

RIEI

利 栄

Died on the fourteenth day of the eighth month, 1794
at the age of twenty-two

All freezes again—	*Uragarete*
among the pines, winds whispering	*kaeru ya matsu ni*
a prayer.	*hannyagoe*

❖

RIFU

梨 風

Died on the sixth day of the tenth month, 1762
past the age of fifty

I'm happy through and through	*Hito-suji ni*
upon a throne	*ureshiki shimo no*
of frost.	*utena kana*

Shimo no utena means "dais of frost." According to Buddhist belief, a dead soul (which has become, by dying, a Buddha) sits in paradise on a lotus seat (*hasu no utena,* lit., lotus calyx). Rifu, who died in the cold season, seems to interweave his last view of this world with the first glimpse of the next.

❖

ROBUN

蘆 文

Died in about 1725

A water bird, asleep,	*Ukine suru*
floats on the river	*tori ya shōji no*
between life and death.	*sakaigawa*

❖

ROCHU

蘆 中

Died on the sixth day of the tenth month, 1744
at the age of forty-four

Is it only me?
Come to think of it, all rests on
pillars of frost.

Ware nomi ka
omoeba shimo no
hashiradate

❖

ROGAN

呂 丸

Died on the second day of the second month, 1693
less than forty years of age

On the ground
around the capital, spring snow
melts easily.

Kieyasushi
miyako no tsuchi zo
haru no yuki

Rogan, a pupil of Basho's, was a resident of the Tohoku
region in the north of Japan. He died in Kyoto during a
springtime journey. In Kyoto, Japan's capital at the time,
spring snow melts sooner than in the north.

❖

ROGEN

露 言

Died on the tenth day of the fourth month, 1691
past the age of sixty

The times are torn asunder—	*Sanze kire*
the half-moon of the past,	*kako no maewa ya*
the moon of summer.	*natsu no tsuki*

Sanze means "three tenses," past, present, and future. *Maewa* is the term for the saddlebow, the front part of the saddle, which resembles a crescent moon. It is possible that the poet is referring to his past journeys on horseback, but in translating I have assumed he had in mind this resemblance of form.

❖

ROKA

浪 化

Died on the ninth day of the tenth month, 1703
at the age of thirty-three

Evening shadows steal	*Tate yoko to*
across and up the folding screen—	*byōbu ni kurete*
a passing winter shower.	*shigure kana*

❖

ROKUSHI

六 之

Died on the sixteenth day of August, 1881
at the age of seventy-five

I wake up	*Awa no meshi*
from a seventy-five-year dream	*samete shichijū*
to millet porridge.	*gonen kana*

The poem alludes to a Chinese folktale about a man who dreamed that he rose in importance and became the holder of a wealthy estate. He woke up to discover that the millet porridge he had put on the fire had not yet boiled. The moral of the story is that visions of grandeur are vain, but it is tinged perhaps with a Zen Buddhist flavor as well: the truth we search for is to be found in the simple things before our eyes.

❖

ROSEN

露 川

Died on the twenty-third day of the eighth month, 1743
at the age of eighty-three

Sweep away	*Hito-taki no*
the pile of ashes	*hai hakinagase*
into autumn waters.	*aki no mizu*

Aki no mizu, "autumn waters," referring to clear waters, indicates the season in which Rosen died.

The poem presents the final act of cleaning the site of his cremation. Rosen prefaced his poem with the words "The soul will return to the sky and the body will dwell in the earth." While this might indicate a belief in the afterlife, it is preferable to understand the phrase as a reference to the dissolution of the elements, each of which separates and returns to its origin.

❖

ROSHU

路　周

*Died on the eighteenth day of May, 1899
at the age of seventy-four*

Time to go . . .	*Tabidachi ya*
they say the journey is a long one:	*tōshi to kiite*
change of robes.	*koromogae*

Koromogae, the change from heavy clothes to light ones, not only fixes the approximate date of Roshu's death between spring and summer, but contains a reference to the white cloth used to wrap the dead in as well. Buddhist monks generally put on a white robe near the hour of their death.

❖

RYOKAN

良　寛

*Died on the sixth day of the first month, 1831
at the age of seventy-four*

Now it reveals its hidden side
and now the other—thus it falls,
an autumn leaf.

Ura o mise
omote o misete
chiru momiji

Ryokan is one of the most well-known of Japan's poets. At
the age of seventeen he left his home and from then until his
death lived as a Zen monk. Most of the time he supported
himself by begging rice from door to door. He was always
content with his lot. At times he would take part in the village
children's games, or gather herbs with the women. Near the
end of his life he became attached to a young Zen nun named
Teishinni, who tended and fed him in his illness. His death
poem may have been composed by another poet; it was
spoken by Ryokan to Teishinni in his last moments.

❖

RYOSA

了 佐

Died on the eleventh day of the seventh month, 1807
at the age of eighty-four

Is man a
morning glory that he passes
in a day?

Sarishi hito wa
kyō o kagiri no
asagao ka

❖

RYOTO

涼 菟

Died on the twenty-eighth day of the fourth month, 1717
at the age of fifty-nine

I understand:	*Gatten ja*
a cuckoo cries	*sono akatsuki no*
today at dawn.	*hototogisu*

The last moments of Ryoto, who served as a Shinto priest and was a disciple of Basho's, are recounted as follows:

When the hour of Ryoto's death approached, he began to say his will. Those standing near his bed asked apprehensively, "Is it fitting that a man like you die without leaving a death poem? . . ." Ryoto opened his eyes and responded, "I understand: / a cuckoo cries / today at dawn." After a moment he went on, "Perhaps I ought to say, '*The* cuckoo cries / today at dawn [*akatsuki no sono* / *hototogisu*].' " Ryoto's pupil Otsuyu, standing at the foot of the bed, said, "What on earth are you thinking about at a time like this? '*A* cuckoo cries / today at dawn' is fine as it stands." Another pupil, Sohoku, took a brush and wrote the poem.[11]

A later source claims that Ryoto died immediately after reciting his poem and denies the exchange between him and Otsuyu. The same source gives a tanka written by Ryoto during his final illness:

Till now	*Ima made wa*
I thought that only	*hito ga shinuru to*
others die—	*omoishi ni*
that such happiness	*waga mi no ue ni*
should fall to me!	*kaku no shiawase*[12]

❖

RYOU

涼 宇

Died on the fifth day of the eleventh month, 1794

A plover rises	*Akatsuki no*
from the waves	*nami ni wakaruru*
at dawn.	*chidori kana*

Chidori is a general name for a number of birds resembling the plover. Certain kinds of *chidori* spend autumn and part of winter in Japan. By day, flocks of these birds fly far out above the sea, returning to spend the night on the beach. The melancholy voice of the plover is mentioned in ancient Japanese literature to evoke the image of winter nights.

❖

RYUHO

立 圃

Died in the ninth month, 1669
at the age of seventy-five

Now I understand how	*Tsuki hana no*
the third verse of moon and flowers	*sanku-me o ima*
is interwoven.	*shiru yo kana*

Ryuho, like many of his generation, participated in writing
renga, or linked verse. To write such a poem, two or more
poets (sometimes as many as twenty or thirty) would take a
part, each poet adding in turn a verse to the preceding one.
By the rules of the art, each verse of poetry had to form a
unit with the preceding and following verses. *Renga* poetry
is full of wit and spirit, and is spiced with puns and double
meanings. Elaborate rules decide just where in the chain
certain seasonal images must appear, as well as the number
of times words such as "moon" or "flower" may be used. By
convention, the third verse of the *renga* must be somewhat
detached from the images of the first and second verse. In
his death poem, Ryuho seems to be alluding to the detach-
ment of the third verse from the preceding ones. The art of
composition in the world of "moon and flower" poetry may
be learned from one's master, but only a man's years can
teach him the art of detachment and ultimate departure.

❖

RYUSAI

笠 斎

Died on the eleventh day of November, 1895
at the age of sixty-five

Brittle pampas grass—
the road
is bright.

Karetogete
michi no akaruki
obana kana

❖

RYUSHI

隆 志

Died on the sixth day of the ninth month, 1764
at the age of seventy

Man is Buddha—
the day and I
grow dark as one.

Mi wa hotoke
ware to iu hi wa
kurenikeri

❖

RYU'U

竜 雨

Died on the third day of December, 1934
at the age of sixty-one

The New Year	*Mayudama ya*
ornaments look hazy—	*kasumu to miete*
snow is on the way.	*yukimoyoi*

Mayudama are small red and white rice-cake balls put on willow branches with other colorful ornaments for New Year's decorations. The custom apparently originated in ancient agricultural rites in which an abundant harvest of cocoons *(mayu)* was prayed for.

❖

SAIBA

西 馬

Died on the fifteenth day of the eighth month, 1858
at the age of fifty-one

I shift my pillow	*Meigetsu no*
closer to the	*hō e korobasu*
full moon.	*makura kana*

Saiba died on the day of the full autumn moon. The poet no doubt refers to the act of moving his bed closer to the window through which the moon is shining.

❖

SAIKAKU

西 鶴

Died on the tenth day of the eighth month, 1693
at the age of fifty-two

In this delusive world	*Ukiyo no tsuki*
I viewed the moon	*misugoshinikeri*
two years too long.	*sue ni-nen*

Ihara Saikaku, a central figure in Japanese literature, is remembered mostly as an author of novels of romance. His works became popular with the common people of Japan and are read and dramatized to this day. A merchant of Osaka and also a haiku poet, Saikaku was of the same generation as Basho, but there is no evidence that the two ever met. In an essay, Basho criticized Saikaku for trying to ingratiate himself with the masses by means of "an inferior style." If Basho holds first place among haiku poets, Saikaku takes honors as the most rapid: in a single-day contest for speed, he is said to have written twenty-three thousand five hundred haiku.

An Oriental belief holds the number of years allotted to man's life as fifty. Saikaku introduces his death poem with these words: "Man's life lasts fifty years. Even that is more than enough for me." *Ukiyo,* "floating world," is the most common epithet given to the world in Japanese. In the traditional Buddhist view, this world is one in which happening gives way to happening, illusion follows illusion, and all of it is nothing but a phantasm void of substance.

❖

SAIKAKU

西 角

Died on the eighth day of the eighth month, 1730
at the age of seventy

I borrow moonlight	*Tsukikage o*
for this journey of a	*katte ima iku*
million miles.	*jūman-ri*

The unit of distance *(ri)* used in this poem is equivalent to about four kilometers. The distance given, a hundred thousand *ri,* is a hyperbolic expression for the journey to the yonder world.

❖

SAIMARO

才 麿

Died on the second day of the first month, 1738
at the age of eighty-three

I'll cross the ridge	*Hirasaka o*
up to the yonder side:	*achira e koseba*
journey into spring.	*haru no tabi*

The ridge here evidently refers to the mountains over which the dead must cross to reach the next world.

❖

SAIMU

西 武

Died in 1679
past the age of seventy

Dawn breaks	*Yo no akete*
and blossoms open	*hana ni hiraku ya*
gates of paradise.	*jōdo mon*

In this poem, night, blossoms, and the gates of paradise are all linked by the verb *hiraku,* "to open," which can refer to the breaking of dawn, the blooming of flowers, and the opening of the gates of paradise.

❖

SAKYOKU

砂 旭

Died on the fifth day of the second month, 1790
at the age of twenty-one

How sad . . .	*Ara kanashi*
amidst the flowers of the spring equinox	*hana no higan o*
a journey deathward.	*shide no tabi*

Sakyoku died on the day of the equinox *(higan)* of spring, a day on which the Japanese hold ceremonies in remembrance of their ancestors. Cherry trees begin to bloom at about this time of year.

❖

SARUO

猿 男

Died on the twenty-seventh day of April, 1923
at the age of sixty-three

Cherry blossoms fall
on a half-eaten
dumpling.

Kuikaketa
dango ni hana no
wakare kana

A *dango* is a rice dumpling, sometimes filled with red-bean paste. One occasion for eating *dango* is during the cherry-blossom season in the spring. *Hana no / wakare* means literally "flower departure"; the expression can be taken to mean the parting between the onlooker and the blossoms. It is perhaps best, however, not to read the viewer into the poem at all, but to take it as the end of a scene in which only a half-eaten dumpling and falling blossoms are left on the stage.

❖

SEIJU

盛 住

*Died on the fifteenth day of the eighth month, 1776
at the age of seventy-five*

Not even for a moment
do things stand still—witness
color in the trees.

*Shibaraku mo
nokoru mono nashi
kigi no iro*

❖

SEIJU

盛 住

*Died on the twenty-eighth day of the eighth month, 1779
at the age of eighty-six*

Water veins
stain rice fields different
shades of green.

*Mizusuji o
ukete kotonaru
aota kana*

In summer, rice seedlings sprout and spread wet green carpets
over the flatlands. Differences in the quality and temperature
of water in the irrigation ditches and in the water flowing
underground beneath the fields result in different shades of
green among the plants.

❖

SEIRA

青 蘿

Died on the seventeenth day of the sixth month, 1791
at the age of fifty-two

Boarding the boat	*Funabata ya*
I slip off my shoes:	*kutsu nugisuteru*
moon in the water.	*mizu no tsuki*

Seira prefaced this poem by saying that he had no further expectation of any man and that, having suffered from inflammation of the skin and a boil the size of a pumpkin on his head (out of which, perhaps, "a boat could be made to return to the land of the dead"), he could no longer escape the inevitable.

❖

SEISA

清 佐

Died on the nineteenth day of the ninth month, 1722
at the age of forty-seven

My body, useless	*Kimamori to*
as the last persimmon	*narite eki naki*
on the tree.	*kono mi kana*

The persimmon tree *(kaki)* usually appears in haiku poetry as an autumnal season word, as its fruit ripens in that season. The word *kaki* is not explicitly mentioned in the poem, but *kimamori,* "tree-preserving talisman," refers to an ancient custom connected with the persimmon in which, during harvest, a single fruit was left on the tree as a tree-preserving charm.

In another rite related to persimmons, one performed to insure an abundant harvest of the fruit, an ax would be struck into the trunk of the persimmon tree on the fifth day of the first month, and a man would address the tree with these words: "Will you bear fruit, or will you not? If you will not, you shall be cut down." Another man would respond for the tree: "I will bear fruit. I will bear." Following this, chopsticks would be inserted into the cut made by the ax and the tree would be "fed" bean paste.

❖

SEISHU

清 秋

Died on the seventeenth day of the fifth month, 1817
at the age of ninety-four

Rain clouds clear away:
above the lotus shines
the perfect moon.

Ame harete
hasu ni shinnyo no
tsukiyo kana

The poem creates an atmosphere of transcendence beyond this world: the lotus is the flower of paradise; "the perfect moon" symbolizes the enlightened mind.

Seishu was a daimyo, the governor of a province. It would not be correct to think he was entirely unworldly throughout his ninety-four years. The sources report that one day, as he was taking a walk, he discovered a broken bridge that had sunk into a river. He removed a plank from the water and made from it a table for himself.

❖

SEMPO

沾 圃

Died on the fourteenth day of the sixth month, 1730

Deep in the underbrush
a cool breeze
sweeps the path.

Oitakete
iru oku suzushi
michi no kaze

❖

SENCHOJO

仙 鳥 女

Died on the sixth day of the fourth month, 1802

I cup my ears
among the deutzia lest I fail
to hear the cuckoo.

Unohana ni
kikisokonawaji
hototogisu

The flowering season of the deutzia, the blossoms of which signal the onset of summer, corresponds to the time when the voice of the cuckoo is most heard. The Japanese word for this flower, *unohana,* is related to that for the fourth month of the lunar calendar, *uzuki,* the first month of summer.

Senchojo was a woman.

❖

SENKEI

仙 径

Died on the twenty-ninth day of the seventh month, 1775
at the age of seventy-one

Somehow or other
even the cactus shows
the fall.

Haōju no
nantomonashi ni
aki kurenu

Haoju, "king of plants," is the name for the prickly-pear cactus. This plant is not common in Japan, and it is not much mentioned in haiku poetry. The cactus is a robust plant which does not change with the seasons as much as other plants.

❖

SENRYU

川　柳

Died on the twenty-third day of the ninth month, 1790
at the age of seventy-three

Bitter winds of winter—	*Kogarashi ya*
but later, river willow,	*ato de me o fuke*
open up your buds.	*kawayanagi*

Senryu was the first to write haiku in the light style named after him. For decades he was esteemed as the foremost haiku critic in Edo. He would rate every haiku presented to him, and those he judged best were published in a series of pamphlets. It is estimated that he criticized about two and a half million poems in his lifetime.

Senryu's name consists of the characters for stream *(sen)* and willow *(ryu)*. These signs appear in his death poem with their Japanese pronunciations, *kawa* and *yanagi*.

❖

SENRYU

川　柳

Died on the seventeenth day of the tenth month, 1818

A willow tree in fall:	*Hana hodo ni*
its leaves will not be missed	*mi wa oshimarezu*
as much as cherry blossoms.	*chiru yanagi*

This Senryu was the eldest son of the previous Senryu and followed him as head of the *senryu* school of poetry. He died shortly after the season in which the willow loses its leaves.

❖

SENRYU

川 柳

Died on the second day of the sixth month, 1827

Like dewdrops	*Hasu no ha no*
on a lotus leaf	*tsuyu to kieyuku*
I vanish.	*wagami kana*

This Senryu was the younger brother of the previous Senryu and succeeded him as head of the *senryu* school.

❖

SENSEKI

荃 石

Died on the twenty-seventh day of the sixth month, 1742
at the age of thirty

At long last I am leaving:	*Tsui ni yuku*
in rainless skies, a cool moon—	*minazuki suzushi*
pure is my heart.	*mune kiyoshi*

Senseki's father was well versed in the secrets of Shinto. Senseki studied Shinto with his father but did not, however, understand it entirely. When his father died, Senseki caught a fatal disease. He felt he could not leave the world without first understanding Shinto thoroughly. He sent for Teisa (p. 323), a friend of his father's who was also learned in religion. Teisa came to Senseki's deathbed and taught him the secret doctrine. At this Senseki's face lit up, he said his death poem and died.

Minazuki is the name of the sixth month of the lunar calendar, which corresponds roughly to July. In Japanese, the word for "month" and "moon" is the same; thus the image of the moon appears in the poem.

❖

SENTOKU

沾 徳

*Died on the thirtieth day of the sixth month, 1726
at the age of sixty-five*

Like ice in storage	*Kowa yoku o*
that will not last	*matanu himuro no*
the year out . . .	*yado narikeri*

The Japanese used to bring ice down from the snow-covered mountains, or cut it from frozen ponds. They put it in caves or icehouses *(himuro)* to keep it through the summer. Blocks of ice were sent from these icehouses to the estates of noble-

men and to the emperor's court. Sentoku, a sword-polisher
by trade, died in the middle of summer.

❖

SETSUDO

雪　堂

Died on the twenty-eighth day of the third month, 1776
at the age of sixty-one

Now then,	*Ima zo kiru*
for my journey to the yonder world	*nori no tabiji no*
I'll wear a gown of flowers.	*hanagoromo*

Hanagoromo, "gown of flowers," is an elegant kimono worn
during the cherry-blossom season in the spring. The expres-
sion is also used in a wider sense for "fancy dress," but Setsu-
do, who died in spring, was no doubt thinking of the cherry
blossoms themselves.

❖

SHAGAI

車　蓋

Died on the twenty-eighth day of the second month, 1795

Reality is flowerlike:
cold clouds sinking through
the dusk.

Hana ni utsutsu
yūbe ni shizumu
kumo samushi

❖

SHARYU

舎 笠

Died on the thirteenth day of the ninth month,
sometime in the middle of the nineteenth century

I have gone through
this world—a life
of moon and snow and flowers.

Yo o heshi mo
tsuki yuki hana no
inochi kana

❖

SHAYO

車 用

Died on the twenty-eighth day of the sixth month, 1776
at the age of fifty-eight

"Hold on!"—
and in the pause,
"Buddha have mercy!"

Dokkoi to
tomatta tokoro de
Namu Amida

This poem presents a struggle between death and the dying, perhaps from the world of *sumo*, Japanese wrestling. *Dokkoi*, which means something like "Hold on!" or "Not so fast!" is a cry which is used to check the opponent's attack. During the moment gained by crying out, the dying uses his last remaining weapon—prayer.

❖

SHIDOKEN

志 道 軒

Died on the seventh day of the third month, 1765

Returning as it came,
a naked summer
worm.

*Sono mama ni
kaeru zo natsu no
hadakamushi*

Hadakamushi (lit., naked worm) is a general term for all hairless worms and crawling insects. The expression is used figuratively for a human or pauper.

❖

SHIEI

子 英

Died on the second day of the sixth month, 1715

Of such a time as this	*Kono toki no*
the proverb speaks:	*sewa o oshie no*
this, too, shall pass.	*mujō kana*

Mujo refers to transcience and is a central principle in Buddhist teaching: the world of appearances lacks permanent substance, and all that one sees passes away as it comes, disappearing into nothingness.

❖

SHIGAN

芝 翫

*Died on the twenty-fifth day of the seventh month, 1838
at the age of sixty-one*

Farewell to "Blessed be"	*Namu saraba*
farewell to the Lotus Sutra—	*Myōhō-Renge*
today, the end.	*kyō kagiri*

The word *kyo* in the original gives rise to a play on words, as it may mean "sutra" or "today." *Namu* means "blessed be," and *Myoho-Renge-kyo* is the Japanese name of the Lotus Sutra (lit., the splendid teaching of the Lotus Sutra). Leaving out *saraba*, "farewell," we get the phrase *Namu Myoho-Renge-kyo*, the opening words of the sutra and a prayer whose recital is a supreme commandment of the Nichiren Buddhist sect. This sutra is a writing of central importance to the

Mahayana branch of Buddhism. It was translated from Sanskrit to Chinese in the first centuries A.D.

Shigan was an actor in the Kabuki theater.

❖

SHIGENOBU

重　信

Died on the twenty-eighth day of the eleventh month, 1832

A willow branch	*Nageire no*
that doesn't reach the water	*mizu mo todokazu*
in the vase.	*yanagi kana*

The imagery of this poem is taken from the world of Japanese flower arrangement. In the *nageire* (lit., throwing in) style, the flowers and branches are set on the lip of a tall vase in an effort to achieve a natural effect. One willow branch, however, may not reach deep enough and is thus cut off from the water in the bottom of the vase, the source of life.

❖

SHIKAKU

紙　隔

Died on the twenty-third day of the ninth month, 1767
at the age of fifty-three

To grass it comes	*Kusa ni kite*
and turns to grass:	*kusa ni kaeru ya*
a drop of dew.	*tsuyu no tama*

❖

SHIKI

子 規

Died on the nineteenth day of September, 1902
at the age of thirty-six

The loofah blooms and	*Hechima saite*
I, full of phlegm,	*tan no tsumarishi*
become a Buddha.	*hotoke kana*

A barrelful of phlegm—	*Tan itto*
even loofah water	*hechima no mizu mo*
will not avail me now.	*ma ni awazu*

Loofah water	*Ototoi no*
from two days ago	*hechima no mizu mo*
left still untouched.	*torazariki*

Shiki is considered the founder of the modern school of haiku. He rejected the poetic tradition begun by Basho and discovered in the haiku of Buson the descriptive style, which he attempted to revive.

Shiki was a journalist, editor, and literary critic. In the early 1890s he was sent to China by his newspaper to cover the

Sino-Japanese War. There he contracted tuberculosis. He returned to Japan, where he was confined to a sickbed for a number of years until his death. Adhering to the principle of the "descriptive style," he depicted the various stages of his illness in poetry. He requested, perhaps to take revenge on his employers, that the words "Journalist. Salary: thirty-five yen" be inscribed on his tombstone.

The poems given here are the last Shiki wrote. All three contain reference to the loofah *(hechima)*, a climbing vine with various practical uses (see p. 255). Loofah sap *(hechima no mizu,* lit., loofah water) is taken as a cough remedy, and it was given for this reason to tuberculosis patients. The sap is customarily pressed from the stalk on the fifteenth of the ninth month, so we can tell that the third poem was written two days before the poet's death. Shiki, knowing that medicine will be of no avail, does not bother to take it.

In the second poem, *itto* means "one *to,*" a unit of volume equivalent to about one hundred eighty liters.

❖

SHIKO

市 貢

Died on the fourth day of the first month, 1743
at the age of fifty-three

I vanish—	*Ware kiete*
in the window	*mado ni nokoru ya*
snows of Eagle Peak remain.	*Washi no yuki*

Shiko lived in the eastern section of Kyoto, in the foothills of the mountain called Washi-ga-mine (lit., Eagle Peak). He died during the height of the snowy season.

❖

SHIKO

市　紅

Died on the sixth day of the sixth month, 1845
at the age of fifty-seven or fifty-eight

A cricket, crying,	*Naku mushi o*
comes with me through	*waga michizure ya*
autumn mountains.	*aki no yama*

Mushi is a general term for insects, but this is an autumn poem, and the insect whose voice fills all Japan throughout this season is the cricket.

"Autumn mountains" *(aki no yama)* refers, perhaps, to the mountains which stand, according to Japanese tradition, between the worlds of the living and the dead.

❖

SHINGA

蓁　峨

Died on the seventh day of the seventh month, 1843

Feast of the Dead:
a fitting time
to die.

Urabon ya
shinde yuku ni wa
yoi jibun

Shinga died six days before the beginning of the Bon Festival, also called Urabon.

❖

SHINSEKI

臣 石

Died on the thirteenth day of the tenth month, 1764
at the age of fifty-two

Fickle winter shower:
up the road comes
an umbrella.

Sadame nashi
shigure no michi no
mukaigasa

❖

SHISUI

之 水

Died on the ninth day of the ninth month, 1769
at the age of forty-four

The following has been written about Shisui's "death poem":

> During his last moments, Shisui's followers requested
> that he write a death poem. He grasped his brush, painted
> a circle, cast the brush aside, and died.[13]

The circle *(enso)* is one of the most important symbols of Zen
Buddhism. It indicates void—the essence of all things—and
enlightenment. There is perhaps a connection between the
figure of a circle and the shape of the full moon, another sym-
bol of enlightenment.

❖

SHIYO

子 葉

*Died on the fourth day of the second month, 1703
at the age of thirty-two*

Surely there's a teahouse
with a view of plum trees
on Death Mountain, too.

*Ume de nomu
chaya mo aru beshi
shide no yama*

Shiyo (Otaka Gengo Tadao) is one of the forty-seven samurai who, in the winter of 1703, avenged the death of their master and who were thus ordered to commit *seppuku* as punishment (see p. 250). In Shiyo's death poem, *shide no yama,* "mountain of death," is the mountain crossed, according to the belief, in the journey from life to death.

It is recorded that Shiyo left another death poem in his last letter to his mother:

Snow on the pines	*Yama no saku*
thus breaks the power	*chikara mo orete*
that splits mountains.	*matsu no yuki*

A poem similar to Shiyo's was written by Kaiga Yazaemon Tomonobu, another of the forty-seven samurai. The similarity between the poems is less, perhaps, a sign of Kaiga's smaller talent than a testimony to the friendship between him and Shiyo:

And won't there be	*Sakura saku*
a teahouse among cherry blossoms	*chaya mo araji na*
along the way of death?	*shide no tabi*

❖

SHIZAN

紫　残

*Died on the tenth day of the third month, 1775
at the age of eighty-four*

Willingly
I fade away within
the heat wave.

*Kagerō to
tomo ni kiyuru zo
kokoroyoki*

Kagero is the term for a natural phenomenon that is characteristic of spring, the season in which Shizan died. As the ground warms up and the air becomes full of vapor, rays from the sun are bent by the heavy air, and things appear to shimmer as if seen through a flame.

❖

SHOFU

椎 風

*Died on the fifth day of the twelfth month, 1848
at the age of fifty-seven*

One moon—
one me—
snow-covered field path.

*Tsuki hitotsu
wagami hitotsu ya
noji no yuki*

❖

SHOGETSU

松 月

*Died on the second day of September, 1899
at the age of seventy*

Autumn ends: *Yuku aki no*
frogs settle down   *tsuchi ni osamaru*
into the earth.   *kawazu kana*

Frogs usually appear in spring or summer poems. Here, however, the season is the end of autumn, and the time is the time of death. Shogetsu fits his imagery to the season, when frogs burrow into the mud to hibernate. The verb *osamaru* means "to become silent" as well as "to settle down."

❖

SHOGO

松 後

*Died on the third day of the fourth month, 1798
at the age of sixty-seven*

Today the sky above Mount Hiei, too, *Hie mo kyō*
takes off its clouds: *kumo naki sora ya*
a change of robe.   *koromogae*

Shogo died at about the time of *koromogae,* the change from heavier clothes to lighter ones.

 Mount Hiei (the short form of whose name is used in the original) is located north of Kyoto, the city in which Shogo died. The mountain is the site of ancient temples.

❖

SHOHAKU

尚 白

Died on the nineteenth day of the seventh month, 1722
at the age of seventy-three

A swollen bottle gourd	*Yūgao no*
dangles from the vine:	*sagari fusube ya*
autumn of my old age.	*oi no aki*

Yesterday, it was hibiscus	*Kinō wa mukuge*
today, my life is	*kyō wa asagao nite*
morning glory.	*kurashikeri*

Shohaku, a doctor, was one of Basho's pupils. His own pupils wrote the following about the poems presented here:

Shohaku wrote these poems during his illness. When he was about to die, he said, "I shall soon abandon the world, and while this is no time to rack my brain for a death poem, I leave these two poems as a legacy of my poetry."[14]

Shohaku's illness was a swelling in his throat, to which the poet is probably referring with "a swollen bottle gourd." Shohaku died the day the growth burst open.

The bottle gourd (*yugao,* lit., evening face) is a climbing vine with pumpkin-like fruit. In summer, toward evening, white flowers blossom; they wither by dawn of the following day. The *mukuge,* a common bush in hedges and gardens, is the rose of Sharon, a species of hibiscus. The plant sports blossoms of various colors at the end of its branches. These flowers, fading in the space of a day, symbolize the ephemeral, as do those of the morning glory, which bloom for only a few hours. Both my youth and my old age, hints the poet, were but episodes that passed like short-lived flowers.

❖

SHOHI

松 琶

*Died on the fourteenth day of the eighth month, 1750
at the age of seventy-nine*

O morning glory—
I, too, yearn for
eternity.

*Asagao ya
ware mo meate wa
jūman'okudo*

Juman'okudo is one of the names for paradise or the eternal; it means literally "the ten trillion land." This might refer to the distance between paradise and this world, but it may also suggest infinite duration.

Although Shohi's poem expresses a desire to abandon this world, it would seem that he was nevertheless quite interested in its phenomena. It is said that while Shohi was visiting the poet Rosen (p. 266) in the city of Nagoya during one of his journeys, he heard that an elephant was being shipped to the shogun in Edo. The fifty-seven-year-old poet became curious. He went forty miles out of his way, lodging overnight in a roadside inn and getting up at three in the morning, just to catch a glimpse of the animal.

❖

SHOKEI

松 逕

*Died on the thirteenth day of February, 1895
at the age of seventy-two*

My shame in this world	*Yo no haji o*
will soon be forgotten—	*kakisute ni shite*
springtime journey.	*haru no tabi*

Bound into this poem is the popular saying *tabi no haji wa kakisute,* "the shame of the journey is soon forgotten." A person who does something unseemly while on a journey is not held responsible for it in the same way that he would be for a deed committed at home. (This saying points out a weakness in Confucian morality, which very strictly defines the duties of an individual toward his permanent environment, but largely neglects the duty owed to strangers away from home.) Shokei quotes the saying almost word for word, but replaces *tabi,* "journey," with *yo,* "this world." His life in this world is thus presented as if he were in a strange land where he feels uprooted from the source of his being; consequently, he need not account for his behavior. The "springtime journey" *(haru no tabi)* is Shokei's journey toward death; he died in the early part of that season.

❖

SHOKU'U

織 雨

Died on the twenty-first day of the eleventh month, 1772
at the age of forty-five

Chilling cold:	*Ura samushi*
winds blow through	*mujō no kaze ni*
bleak timber.	*teranu ki mo*

❖

SHORO

蕉 露

Died in April, 1894
at the age of eighty

Pampas grass, now dry,	*Samazama ni*
once bent this way	*soyogitsukushite*
and that.	*kareobana*

❖

SHOSHUN

正 春

Died on the twenty-fourth day of the fourth month, between 1660 and 1672
less than ninety years of age

Flowers bloomed yesterday,
today winds blow—
what but a dream . . .

Yume nare ya
hana wa sakujitsu
kyō no kaze

❖

SHOZAN

松　山

Died on the third day of the tenth month, 1873

The fall of leaves
has left some autumn
on the lower branches.

Shita-eda ni
aki o nokoshite
ochiba kana

In 1873 the Japanese lunar calendar was replaced by the Gregorian, but some sources continued to give dates in the old system for a time. If the date of Shozan's death is computed by the new calendar, it appears that he died in the middle of November, at the close of autumn.

Trees shed their leaves from top to bottom, and at the end of autumn a few leaves can be found still clinging to lower branches.

❖

SHUHO

舟　甫

Died in 1767

Cicada shell:
little did I know
it was my life.

Mi no ue to
shirazu ni semi no
monuke kana

❖

SHUKABO

秋 果 坊

Died on the eighth day of the eleventh month, 1775
at the age of fifty-eight

Is it me the raven calls
from the world of shades
this frosty morning?

Ware o yobu ka
meido mo shimo no
asagarasu

Meido, "dark land," is a term for the land of the dead. The
boundary between this world and the next has been blurred
in the poem.

❖

SHUKYO

秋 挙

Died on the twenty-fifth day of the seventh month, 1826

Above the fence	*Asagao no*
a morning glory stretches	*matamata taranu*
still unsatisfied.	*kakine kana*

It seems that the morning glory, like man, is never satisfied with its lot, and when it reaches the top of the fence along which it climbs, it keeps shooting upward where there is nothing to support it.

❖

SHUMPAN

春 帆

Died in about the second month, 1703
at the age of thirty-four

The winter fowl	*Kanchō no*
ends up with feathers	*mi wa mushiraruru*
plucked.	*yukue kana*

Shumpan (Tomimori Suke'emon Masayori) was one of the forty-seven samurai who avenged the death of their master and were thus ordered to commit *seppuku* (see p. 250). The poet takes leave of the world with a hunting image. In the tradition of *seppuku*, the victim plunges a dagger into his abdomen; someone else, standing above the victim, strikes off his head with a "mercy blow."

❖

SHUSHIKI

秋 色

*Died on the fifteenth day of the fourth month, 1725
at the age of fifty-seven*

I wake and find	*Mishi yume no*
the colored iris	*sametemo iro no*
I saw in my dream.	*kakitsubata*

Shushiki, a well-known haiku poet, was born into a family with a cake-baking business. She married into a family which dealt in antiques and second-hand goods.

Shushiki's poem reflects a viewpoint of the Mahayana branch of Buddhism, of which Sino-Japanese Buddhism is a part, as opposed to that of the older Theravada branch. Theravada doctrine views enlightenment as an awakening from the world of phenomena, called "color" in Buddhist literature, to the world of truth, the void (nirvana). According to the Mahayana school, the void should not be thought of as a state in itself standing opposite the world of phenomena. Rather, the form of everything around us is the void, and the void is the world in all its shapes and colors. In Shushiki's poem, she awakens from the dream world of colored irises into the world of truth, and there, too, irises are found.

The iris *(kakitsubata)* grows beside lakes and marshes to a height of fifty to seventy centimeters. The wild iris blooms in May and June with deep purple flowers; the flowers of the domesticated variety may be white as well.

❖

SHUTEI

秋 亭

*Died on the twenty-first day of the sixth month, 1858
at the age of forty-eight or forty-nine*

Frost on a summer day: *Fude sosogu*
all I leave behind is water   *mizu mo nagori ya*
that has washed my brush.   *natsu no shimo*

The following has been written about Shutei:

Shutei's father was a *taikomochi* [lit., drum-carrier; a
kind of male geisha who entertained guests in teahouses].
From his childhood Shutei loved to draw. He became
a pupil of the artist Ueda Kocho and was praised for his
mastery of his teacher's style. When his own paintings
did not sell, however, he gave up on them and became
an entertainer in the southern part of Osaka. His painter
friends criticized him harshly for this, and his master even
ostracized him from their company, but Shutei paid them
no mind and continued to be an entertainer. Shutei's
lively paintings were well-liked by his contemporaries.[15]

"Frost on a summer day" *(natsu no shimo)* symbolizes the
ephemeral.

❖

SOA

宋 阿

*Died on the sixth day of the sixth month, 1742
at the age of sixty-six*

Whether or not a paradise	*Koshiraete*
awaits in the far reaches	*aru to mo shirazu*
of the west . . .	*nishi no oku*

Soa was also known by the name Hajin.

❖

SODO

素 堂

*Died on the fifteenth day of the eighth month, 1716
at the age of seventy-five*

Full autumn moon:	*Ware o tsurete*
my shadow takes me with him	*waga kage kaeru*
and returns.	*tsukimi kana*

Sodo died on the day of the full autumn moon.

❖

SOFU

素 風

*Died on the twenty-fourth day of May, 1891
at the age of sixty*

Festival of Souls:	*Tamamatsuri*
yesterday I hosted them	*kinō wa aruji*
today I am a guest . . .	*kyō wa kyaku*

Tamamatsuri, the Festival of Souls, is another name for the Bon Festival.

❖

SOHOKU

曽 北

*Died on the fifth day of the second month, 1743
at the age of sixty-four*

Empty are	*Kūkū to*
the smells of things . . .	*mono no nioi ya*
moon above plum blossoms.	*tsuki no ume*

Sohoku died in the spring during the plum-blossom season. It is said that he was a humble and modest man and did not want to take money for teaching haiku. As he was very poor, his pupils built a house for him. During the last winter of his life, he apparently felt his end was near and wrote:

This winter	*Kono fuyu wa*
the willow will freeze	*makoto ni karuru*
for good.	*yanagi kana*

❖

SOKIN

素 琴

Died in 1818

The road I take	*Yuku michi wa*
to paradise is bright	*hana ni akaruki*
with flowers.	*jōdo kana*

"Flowers" *(hana)* usually refers to cherry blossoms in spring. We do not know, however, what season Sokin died in, and it is possible that he meant the lotus, the flower of paradise.

❖

SOKO

鼠 公

*Died on the twenty-fifth day of the eighth month, 1770
at the age of forty-four*

Like full, plump	*Nashi no mi no*
pear flesh	*marumaru to shite*
dwindling away . . .	*hatenikeri*

The *nashi* is a pear-like fruit that has been cultivated in Japan since ancient times. It appears in haiku as a seasonal image for autumn, when its fruit ripens. This was the season of Soko's death as well. The "pear" in this poem refers to the ripened fruit: bitten away by the teeth, or pecked at by birds, it eventually disappears. We may even surmise that Soko himself was overweight.

❖

SOKO

桑 古

Died on the third day of April, 1897
at the age of seventy

Shadows from a lingering sun	*Osoki hi no*
blur into dusk—	*kage mo haya nashi*
falling cherry petals.	*chiru sakura*

"Shadows from a lingering sun" (the time when days grow longer) and "falling cherry petals" are both images that signify the season of spring, when Soko died.

❖

SOMARU

素 丸

*Died on the twentieth day of the seventh month, 1795
at the age of eighty-three*

A green gourd	*Aohisago*
swells and swells and finally—	*fukururu hate ya*
clear autumn waters.	*aki no mizu*

Somaru's death poem appeared in a collection of poetry entitled *Aohisago* (The green gourd), published on the seventeenth anniversary of his death. The poem is prefaced with the words "Before his death his entire body grew swollen."

❖

SONOME

園 女

*Died on the twentieth day of the fourth month, 1726
at the age of seventy-four*

Skies at dawn—	*Akebono no*
is this reality?	*sora wa utsutsu ka*
O God.	*Amida Butsu*

Sonome was a friend of Basho's. When she came to learn

haiku from him in 1690, he wrote a poem comparing her to plum blossoms. Thirteen days before his death in 1694, Basho dedicated another poem to her, describing her as a "pure white chrysanthemum." Sonome's husband, a doctor, died in 1703; in 1718, eight years before her own death, Sonome withdrew into a monastery. It is said that, out of respect for her family, who worshiped Shinto gods, she did not complete the rite required of Buddhist nuns: rather than shave her head completely, she left ten hairs on it.

❖

SO'OKU

宋 屋

Died on the twelfth day of the third month, 1766
at the age of seventy-nine

Walking westward,	*Nishi e yuku*
early cherry blossoms are	*higan sakura ya*
my landmark.	*michi-annai*

So'oku died near the time of the spring equinox. *Higan sakura* (or *higanzakura*), "equinox cherry," is a tall variety of cherry tree with scarlet blossoms that bloom before those of other kinds of cherry, around the time of the equinox.

❖

SORYU

素 柳

*Died in 1797
past the age of seventy*

Autumn winds:
having sworn to save all souls,
I am at peace.

*Akikaze ya
hiroki chikai no
kokoroyoki*

Hiroki chikai, "wide vow," refers to the oath of a bodhisattva, one who strives to enlighten and redeem not only himself, but all men. In the Mahayana tradition, the oath means that the believer unites his aspiration to the world of the absolute with action in this world.

❖

SOSEN

宗 専

*Died on the twenty-eighth day of the sixth month, 1776
at the age of eighty-two*

Lotus seeds
jump every which-way
as they wish.

*Hasu no mi no
tobitokoro ari
shinjizai*

❖

SUGETSU

嵩　月

Died on the twentieth day of the eleventh month, 1830

The years have piled up	*Tsumu toshi ni*
snow on withered fields	*tabiji e yuki no*
along my path.	*kareno kana*

❖

SUIKOKU

水　国

*Died on the eighth day of the fifth month, 1734
at the age of fifty-three*

By the fifth month	*Satsuki kinu*
one has had his fill	*hito mo yanagi ni*
of seeing willows.	*umishi koro*

The willow tree usually appears in haiku as an image of spring. Suikoku died during the gloomy rainy season of early summer.

According to old sources, Suikoku loved not only poetry, but women as well. He fell in love with a famous geisha, ransomed her from her geisha house, and married her. The assets of his tool-making firm dwindled, apparently as a result of his frivolity, and he was forced by the managers to transfer his authority to his daughter.

❖

SUNAO

寸 七 翁

Died in 1926
at the age of thirty-nine

Spitting blood
clears up reality
and dream alike.

Chi o hakeba
utsutsu mo yume mo
saekaeru

❖

TADATOMO

忠 知

Died on the twenty-seventh day of the eleventh month, 1676
at the age of fifty-two

This frosty month
nought but the shadow
of my corpse remains.

Shimotsuki ya
aru wa nakimi no
kagebōshi

Tadatomo committed suicide in the traditional Japanese
manner. The reason for his suicide is not clear. Just before
his death he wrote this death poem and added the words,
"the vicissitudes of my life—how sad!"[16]

Shimotsuki, "frost month," is the name for the eleventh month of the lunar calendar (by the solar calendar, approximately the month of January).

❖

TAIKYO

太 喬

Died in the fourth month, 1770

The deutzia has bloomed—
it's time to start
for those clear western skies.

*Unohana ya
akaruki nishi e
iza ikamu*

❖

TAIRYU

大 立

*Died on the twenty-sixth day of the fourth month, 1747
at the age of sixty-nine*

Flowers bloom a score of days—
I threescore years and nine,
and now dawn breaks.

*Hana wa hatsuka
ware wa rokujūkyū
yoru no ake*

❖

TAKAO

高 尾

Died on the twenty-fifth day of the twelfth month, 1660

Brittle autumn leaves	*Samukaze ni*
that crumble in the	*moroku kuzururu*
north wind . . .	*momiji kana*

Takao is not only the poet's pen name, but her geisha title as well. In the seventeenth and eighteenth centuries the brothel districts of Japan flourished under government supervision. "Takao" was the highest (and most expensive) rank of geisha. The poet belonged to the famous geisha house Miuraya in the Yoshiwara.

Samukaze means "cold wind." In haiku this is a synonym for the north wind. In Japan, summer winds usually blow from the south and winter winds from the north.

❖

TAKUCHI

卓 池

Died on the twenty-first day of the eighth month, 1846
at the age of seventy-nine

When summoned,	*Iza saraba*
I will say farewell:	*mukai shidai ni*
my house beneath the moon.	*tsuki no yado*

❖

TAKURO

卓 郎

Died on the sixteenth day of the fourth month, 1866
at the age of sixty-nine

Soon I shall hear	*Yagate kiku*
the cuckoo's voice	*hitokoe ureshi*
and liven up.	*hototogisu*

Takuro, who was also called Kosando, was known for his miserliness. His acquaintances made slight changes in his two names and combined them in the phrase *yokasando buttakuro,* which means in common speech, "I don't give; I take!"

❖

TAMANARI

玉 成

Died in the fifth month
past the age of sixty

Cool—	*Suzushisa ya*
a seagull suddenly	*pokuri kakururu*
submerges.	*miyakodori*

The year of Tamanari's death is unknown.

❖

TAMASHICHI

玉 七

Died in 1910

A lone monk
came to call
one autumn evening.

Sō hitori
tazunete kitari
aki no kure

❖

TANEHIKO

種 彦

Died on the thirteenth day of the seventh month, 1842
at the age of sixty

Such is the world's way:
in fall the willow
sheds its leaves.

Chiru mono to
sadamaru aki no
yanagi kana

❖

TANKO

旦 藁

Died in 1735(?)
at the age of about seventy

Today too,
melon-cool, the moon
comes up above the fields.

Kyō wa nao
makuwa to suzushi
hata no tsuki

Life-cutting axe:
lured by the hunter's
deer call, a doe approaches.

Inochi tatsu
ono zo na ga yoru
ojikabue

The moon leaks out
from sleeves of cloud
and scatters shadows.

Kage nuguu
tsuki ya morederu
kumo no sode

The first snow
falls upon the bowels
of Tombstone Mountain.

Hatsu-yuki ni
nado fugawari no
Toribe-yama

Tanko, one of Basho's pupils, was a cake-seller and practitioner of acupuncture. Once a sack of grain was brought to Tanko as a present from one of his patients. Tanko was so delighted that he brought out a bottle of rice wine to celebrate the occasion. Just then a messenger came from the sender to inform him that a mistake had been made: the gift that was meant for Tanko was a sack of radishes, not of grain. Tanko was crestfallen. Later, however, when his poet-friend Etsujin came by, the two of them broke out laughing. On another occasion, during an acupuncture treatment, Tanko was unable to extract one of the needles from the body of his patient. Leaving the patient with the needle still in his flesh, he fled from the place.

We do not know when Tanko died. The poems were written a short time before his death, and the seasonal images belong to the time between autumn and winter. The "deer call" in the second poem refers to an instrument blown by hunters which imitates the mating call made by stags in autumn to attract does. Toribe-yama (fourth poem) is the name of a hill in Kyoto that has a cemetery on it.

❖

TANKO

淡 行

Died on the twenty-seventh day of March, 1884
at the age of fifty-eight

For eight and fifty years	*Tsuki hana ni*
I've had my fun	*gojūhachi-nen*
with moon and flowers.	*asobikeri*

❖

TANTAN

淡 々

Died on the second day of the eleventh month, 1761
at the age of eighty-eight

With my cane	*Asashimo ya*
I trace Mount Fuji	*tsue de egakishi*
in the morning frost.	*Fuji-no-yama*

Tantan was considered greedy for wealth and fame by his contemporaries. He lived in Osaka, but it is said he claimed that the water of Osaka was dirty. One of his pupils, the son of a rich family who owned merchant ships, brought Tantan fresh drinking water daily from Kyoto.

❖

TEIKITSU

貞 橘

Died on the eighth day of the eighth month, 1760

Open the shutters	*Mado akeyo*
to the autumn typhoon—	*nori no tsukai no*
herald from beyond.	*akitsumuji*

❖

TEISA

貞 佐

Died on the sixth day of the twelfth month, 1747
at the age of sixty-eight

A plover wades through	*Ato wa mizu*
shallows of the last month	*toshi-no-se o iku*
without turning back.	*chidori kana*

Toshi-no-se, "shallows of the year," is a term referring to the end of the year, when Teisa died. *Toshi* also refers to a person's age.

❖

TEISHI

定 之

Died on the sixth day of the ninth month, 1700
at the age of fifty

A morning glory—
yet how long it stayed alive!
full fifty years.

Asagao wa
hisashiki mono yo
gojū-nen

❖

TEISHITSU

貞 室

Died on the seventh day of the second month, 1673
at the age of sixty-four

New year—
what binds it to my life is
rice gruel.

Kuru toshi no
omoyu ni tsunagu
inochi kana

Teishitsu was unlike other people even as a child. He was a

connoisseur of various arts, he knew history well, and he was a "general" in the ranks of haiku poets. He would often tell ancient tales of heroism, accompanying himself on the *biwa*. When flowers opened up at dawn in the spring, on moon-lit nights in autumn, or early in the morning of new-fallen snow, he would wander to scenic places, plucking the *biwa* or playing the flute.

In the winter of 1672 the poet became ill, and during the new year, a month before his death, he composed the haiku given above. It is not a death poem, but it is rather better than the actual death poem that Teishitsu left behind. The latter is a tanka in which he greets death and informs him that, since the years of his life have been "eight times eight," he has no cause to complain.

❖

TEMBO

天 姥

Died in the eighth month, 1823
at the age of eighty-three

I wish this body
might be dew in a field
of flowers.

Hana no negai
hanano no tsuyu to
naru mi kana

In the original, the wish is made by the flower, but the intention is to the wish of the poet, whose life is compared to a flower. The sources say that when Tembo was seventy-five years old, a rumor spread that he had died. When he heard of this, he said, "Nothingness is but a change in being, and 'departure' means 'meeting'; that is the way of heaven." To commemorate his "death," he published a book of his poetry, and changed his name to Rio, "old pear."

❖

TESSHI

轍 土

Died in 1707

Among the barley stalks	*Mugi no ho ni*
an old fox	*o o kakusaba ya*
hides its tail.	*oigitsune*

Tesshi was notorious for his mocking commentaries on contemporary poets, whom he compared to prostitutes. The harshness of his criticism angered even his best friend, the poet Kikaku.

❖

TESSHU

鉄 舟

Died on the sixth day of the sixth month, 1775
at the age of fifty-two

When I leave
these eyes of flesh, I wish to see
the lotus.

Nikugan o
hanarete mitashi
hasu no hana

❖

TOGYU

都 牛

Died on the fifteenth day of the eighth month, 1749
at the age of forty-four

When autumn winds blow
not one leaf remains
the way it was.

Nan no mama
nokoru ha mo nashi
aki no kaze

❖

TOHO

土 芳

Died on the eighteenth day of the first month, 1730
at the age of seventy-four

Food is steaming
on the stove—
ah, misery . . .

Aware naru
aji atatamaru
hioke kana

A *hioke* (or *hibachi*) is a traditional heater made of wood, metal, or pottery in which charcoal is burned. People gather around the *hioke* in winter to warm themselves and sometimes to heat their food.

Toho was born to a family of rice merchants, but was adopted at an early age by a samurai, an artist in dagger warfare, who taught the art to him. Toho was a native of the same district as Basho, but younger than him by thirteen years. Basho met Toho when the latter was only nine years old; the next time he saw him was twenty years later. On this occasion Basho wrote the following poem "in honor of an old friend after twenty years":

Within your life and mine	*Inochi futatsu*
there lives	*naka ni ikitaru*
a cherry blossom.	*sakura kana*

❖

TOJAKU

都 雀

Died on the eighth day of the eleventh month, 1799

I go back	*Mu ni kaeru*
to the void where frost and snow	*mi zo yuki shimo no*
won't bother me.	*itoi nashi*

Tojaku died in winter, the image of which appears by means of the negation of the attributes of that season.

❖

TOJUN

東　順

*Died on the twenty-ninth day of the eighth month, 1695
at the age of seventy-three*

Even dew distilled
from a thousand herbs
can't cure this illness.

*Shishō ni wa
chikusa no tsuyu no
gen mo nashi*

Tojun, the father of the poet Kikaku, was a doctor. He prefaced his death poem with these words: "A seventy-three year-old doctor cooks up many different brews for himself."

❖

TOKO

杜　口

*Died on the eleventh day of the second month, 1795
at the age of eighty-six*

Death poems
are mere delusion—
death is death.

*Jisei to wa
sunawachi mayoi
tada shinan*

❖

TOKUGEN

徳 元

*Died on the twenty-eighth day of the eighth month, 1647,
at the age of eighty-nine*

My life was
lunacy until
this moonlit night.

*Ima made wa
iki tawagoto o
tsuku yo kana*

Tsuku means both "to talk" (when it accompanies a word
such as *tawagoto*, gibberish) and "moon" (in classical Japanese).

❖

TOMOEMON

友右衛門

Sound of a melody:
thus begins my debut
in the world beyond.

*Ongaku no
koe wa anoyo no
hatsu-yagura*

Tomoemon belonged to the third generation of a family of
actors. He drew from his experience as a Kabuki actor for the
imagery of this poem: *hatsu-yagura* is the drumbeat that marks
the beginning of a play. It is not known when Tomoemon
died.

❖

TOYOKUNI

豊 国

Died on the seventh day of the first month, 1825

Is it like
a charcoal sketch—
a hazy shadow?

*Yakifude no
mama ka oboro ni
kagebōshi*

Yakifude, is a stick singed at one end and used as a brush for charcoal drawings. An artist may trace over these faint lines with brush and ink when making an ink drawing, but the charcoal drawing is a medium in its own right.

❖

UKO

羽 紅

*Died on the third day of the intercalary month, 1743
at the age of fifty-seven*

Cuckoo,
take me up to where
clouds drift.

*Yuku kumo ni
made tsuredatan
hototogisu*

Uko died in the intercalary month added after the fourth
lunar month of 1743. When this date is calculated by the
Gregorian calendar, it appears that he died in summer, the
season of the cuckoo.

❖

UKO

宇 考

*Died on the seventh day of the third month, 1820
at the age of eighty-two*

The voice of the nightingale	*Uguisu no*
makes me forget	*naku ya wasururu*
my years.	*waga yowai*

Old sources tell us that Uko became paralyzed in his old age
and was confined to his bed. On the last day of the second
month, 1820, the lord of his province sent him a gift of wine.
Uko held a banquet and, with a shaking hand, took up his
brush and wrote the poem above, prefacing it with the words
"I received your gift of wine with gratitude." This was his
last poem.

The *uguisu*, the Japanese nightingale, or bush warbler,
frequents the dwellings of man at the end of winter, an-
nouncing the coming of spring.

❖

UNREI

雲 鈴

Died on the second day of the second month, 1717

The second of the second month: *Degawari wa*
a change of servants   *anoyo mo nigatsu*
in the other world as well.   *futsuka kana*

In accordance with a centuries-old tradition, servants of rich houses and commercial firms worked on the basis of half-year contracts. The dates for renewal of the contracts were, in most parts of Japan, the second of the second month and the second of the eighth month. At these times many servants would return to their own homes, and others would come to take their places, a practice called *degawari* (or *dekawari*). The first of these days, in the second month, is a spring season-word in haiku, and Unrei, who died on the day itself, extends the image of servants leaving their establishments to his own exit from this world to the next.

Unrei's death is described thus:

Unrei, a samurai by origin, abandoned society and took to wandering up and down Japan. He studied haiku under Shiko. After some time he built a hut in the village of Izumozaki, in the province of Echigo [present-day Niigata Prefecture], where he taught haiku to the people of the place. There he drank wine, learned to observe the vanities of the world, and abstained from eating cereal crops. When he decided that he had lived long enough, he requested his friends to build for him a coffin. On the second day of the second month, Unrei rose up in the morning, shaved his head, bathed, changed his clothing, and said, "Today there is a good reason to prepare a feast for everyone." He ate and drank with his friends, and in the middle of the celebration said, "And now I shall get inside this casket, so as to put in practice all I have learned during my life. When my breathing ceases, you take care of the rest." He read a short will, and on the paper of this document he wrote his death poem. . . . Those who were with him did not believe him. They thought he was drunk, and some of them even joked, "If it is so easy to abandon this world, then let's all go!" However, about noon, Unrei stopped breathing, and he died leaning on a column, his face flushed with wine, in the attitude of sleep. His friends buried him in Izumozaki.[17]

❖

USEI

雨 声

*Died on the seventh day of the seventh month, 1764
at the age of sixty-six*

Six and sixty—
setting sail in tranquil water,
breeze among the lotus.

*Rokujūroku
defune wa yasushi
hasu no kaze*

In Usei's death poem, the poet's voice becomes that of a pilot steering the ship of life. He announces the time of the voyage —sixty-six (years of life)—the state of the water as the ship leaves harbor, and that of the wind blowing through the lotus leaves in the lake of the afterlife.

❖

UTSU

右　通

*Died on the twenty-fourth day of the second month, 1863
at the age of fifty*

The owner of the cherry blossoms	*Ki no moto no*
turns to compost	*koyashi tomo nare*
for the trees.	*hana no nushi*

Utsu died in spring during the cherry-blossom season.

❖

WAGIN

和　吟

*Died on the third day of the first month, 1758
at the age of seventy-three*

New Year's dawn:	*Kuse ni natte*
but I'm already used to	*nishi ogamikeri*
bowing westward.	*hatsu–ashita*

Wagin died two days after the first dawn of the new year. In a ceremony whose origin apparently lies in the Shinto religion, the Japanese bow to the first rays of the sun of every new year. Wagin, a Buddhist used to bowing to the west toward paradise, now turns his back on the rising sun. He thus hints, with a wry smile, that he already belongs more to the next world than to this one.

❖

WAKYU

和 及

Died on the sixteenth day of the first month, 1692
at the age of forty-four

My four and forty years	*Waga toshi no*
bloom in the last verse	*yoyoshi no hana no*
of a chain poem.	*ageku kana*

By convention, the last verse *(ageku)* of a *renga* contains a spring season-word. Wakyu compares his forty-four year-long life to a chain of poetry which he ends with an image of spring.

❖

WAKYU

和 及

Died on the tenth day of the eleventh month, 1759

In the end	*Tsui ni yuku*
I plow through heavy snow:	*yuki fumiwakete*
the way of the brush.	*fude no michi*

Wakyu died in the winter, and here likens his coming journey to tramping through the snow *(yuki fumiwakete)*. This line is also pivotal, in that Wakyu seems to be saying that his life as a haiku poet, a follower of the "way of the brush" *(fude no michi)*, has been as difficult as the journey upon which he will be soon embarking.

❖

YABA

野 坡

*Died on the third day of the first month, 1740
at the age of seventy-eight*

A voice calls me—	*Ware o yobu*
a sudden winter shower	*koe ya ukiyo no*
in this floating world.	*kata shigure*

Before his death, Yaba is said to have written two poems. The poem above is the first of these two. His very last poem is not clear and is not as good a farewell poem as the one given here.

❖

YAITSU

野　逸

Died on the fifteenth day of the first month, 1807
at the age of eighty

I pass beneath	*Shimekazari*
the New Year's gates—moon in	*kugureba tsuki no*
the skies	
of paradise.	*jōdo kana*
Paradise—	*Waga io ni*
I see flowers	*nete hana o miru*
from the cottage where I lie.	*jōdo kana*

Shimekazari is the name for ornaments made of twisted rope
hung on the gates of houses during the New Year's holidays.
On the fifteenth day of the first month (the day on which
Yaitsu died), the decorations are removed and burned.

Yaitsu prefaced the second poem with the words "The land
of life is the land of everlasting light"—that is, there is no
difference between this world and that of eternity.

❖

YAOHIKO

八 百 彦

Died on the twentieth day of the third month, 1777
at the age of eighty-one

Clouds of flowers
fall not knowing
east or west.

Higashi e mo
nishi e mo yukaji
hana no kumo

Hana no kumo, "clouds of flowers," is a common metaphor for falling cherry petals. Yaohiko, who died around the cherry-blossom season, prefers death after the manner of flowers, whose petals are blown by the wind in all directions, to that of man, who tends only westward, the direction of the Buddhist paradise.

❖

YAYU

也 有

Died on the sixteenth day of the sixth month, 1783
at the age of eighty-two

A short night
wakes me from a dream
that seemed so long.

Mijikayo ya
ware ni wa nagaki
yume samenu

It is said that Yayu had many pastimes. In addition to writing poetry, he painted, fought with swords, and played the *biwa*. He was fond of wine, tobacco, and human company. As a poet, he did not confine himself to haiku: he was known as an artist in *haibun* (prose written using the techniques of haiku), tanka, *kyoka,* and Chinese poetry. It is no wonder, then, that Yayu did not rest content with a haiku death poem only, but added two others, one tanka and one Chinese poem:

Yesterday? Today?	*Kinō kyō to*
Thus death revolved within my thoughts	*omoitsutsu karushi*
and fruitless days wore on—	*mi no hodo zo*
many indeed have been	*nakanaka nagaki*
the years I've lived through.	*yo wa kazoenuru*

*　*　*　*

My sickness lingers; I part from this world.
For many years I hid myself in my village.
From a dream of eighty years and more
I wake at dawn to peals of temple bells.

❖

ZAISHIKI

在 色

*Died on the fifteenth day of the ninth month, 1719
at the age of seventy-seven*

Frost on grass:
a fleeting form
that is, and is not!

*Kusa no shimo
tōza bakari zo
shiraururi*

❖

❖ NOTES ❖

PART ONE

1. Kenneth Yasuda, *The Japanese Haiku* (Rutland and Tokyo: Charles E. Tuttle, 1957), 30–31.

2. Basil Hall Chamberlain, trans., *The Kojiki: Records of Ancient Matters* (1919; reprint, Rutland and Tokyo: Charles E. Tuttle, 1981), 39.

3. Norimoto Yoshihiro, *Nihonjin no Shiseikan* (Tokyo: Kokuminsha, 1944).

4. Chamberlain, *The Kojiki*, 271.

5. *Ibid.*, 371.

6. *Ibid.*, 263.

7. Nishimura Hakucho, *Enka Kidan* (Strange tales of smoke and mist; ghost stories and historical notes) (1773).

8. *Ibid.*

9. *Ibid.*

10. Muju, comp., *Shasekishu* (Collection of sand and stone; narratives illustrating the teachings of Buddhism) (1299).

11. Matsu'ura Seizan, *Kasshi Yawa* (Tales told at night; anecdotes on shogun and daimyo of the Edo period) (drafted *c.* 1828; Tokyo: Koku-shokan Kokai, 1910).

12. Yoel Hoffmann, trans., *Radical Zen: The Sayings of Joshu* (Brookline, Mass.: Autumn Press, 1978), 46, 81, 157.

13. Yoel Hoffmann, trans., *The Sound of the One Hand* (New York: Bantam, 1977), 113.

343

14. *Nomori no Kagami* (The field watchman's mirror; a review of poetry) (fifteenth cent.).

15. Ban Kokei, *Kanden Jihitsu* (Fallow-field essays, continued; miscellaneous essays) (1806).

16. Okanishi Ichu, *Ichijiken Zuihitsu* (Miscellaneous essays of Ichijiken [the author's pen name]) (1683).

17. Ban, *Kanden Jihitsu.*

18. Matsu'ura, *Kasshi Yawa.*

19. *Ibid.*

20. Ban, *Kanden Jihitsu.*

21. Takakuwa Ranko, *Haikai Sesetsu* (*Haikai* opinion; anecdotes about Basho and his disciples) (1785).

22. Natsume Seibi, *Zuisai Kaiwa* (Talks on *haikai* by Zuisai [the author's pen name]) (1819).

23. Okanishi, *Ichiji Zuihitsu.*

24. Nishimura, *Enka Kidan.*

25. Takahashi Yoshitaka, *Shi to Nihonjin* (Death and the Japanese) (Tokyo: Paburishitii, 1959), 48.

26. Nakamura Hajime, lecture at The Japan Society, New York, February 12, 1979; printed in *The Japan Foundation Newsletter,* June/July 1979.

27. Momoi Tou, *Kyuai Zuihitsu* (Essays from a dusty pannier; tales and observations) (*c.* 1789).

PART THREE

1. Takakuwa, *Haikai Sesetsu.*

2. Hayakawa Joseki, comp., *Haikai Kafu* (*Haikai* geneology) (1751).

3. *Ibid.*

4. Takarai Kikaku, *Zotanshu* (Miscellany; prose written using the techniques of haiku [*haibun*]) (1692).

5. Hirose Jikko, comp., *Haikai Kafu Goshui* (More gleanings from *Haikai Kafu*) (1797).

6. Yamamoto Kakei, *Aranoshu* (Wilderness collection; a *haikai* anthology) (1689).

7. Takarai Kikaku, *Hanatsumi* (Flower picking; a *haikai* diary) (1690).

8. Ishida Mitaku, *Hitomotogusa* (One blade of grass; a *haikai* anthology) (1669).

9. Naoe Mokudo, *Mizu no Oto* (The sound of water; a *haikai* anthology) (1723).

10. Takarai, *Zotanshu*.

11. Takebe Ryotai, *Basho-o Zuda Monogatari* (Tales of Master Basho's begging sack; anecdotes about Basho and his disciples) (1751).

12. Takakuwa, *Haikai Sesetsu*.

13. Hirose Jikko, comp., *Haikai Kafu Shui* (Gleanings from *Haikai Kafu*) (1771).

14. Saida and Ennyu, comps., *Yugao no Uta* (Song of the bottle gourd; a *haikai* anthology) (1722).

15. Kamata Haruo, *Kinki Bosekiko* (A study of tombs in the Kinki region) (Osaka: Daitokaku, 1922), 260.

16. Takarai, *Zotanshu*.

17. Kagami Shiko, comp., *Wakan Bunso* (a collection of short pieces of prose and poetry with commentary) (1727).

❖ BIBLIOGRAPHICAL NOTES ❖

To the best of my knowledge, no exhaustive research on the subject of death poems has been written in Japan. The book that comes closest is *Shi no Nihon Bungakushi* (Death in the history of Japanese literature) by Muramatsu Go (Tokyo: Kadokawa Bunko, 1981). This is a detailed study of Japanese attitudes toward death and the reflection of these attitudes in different periods of Japanese literature. However, in the area of poetry the book deals mainly with tanka, scarcely touching upon haiku and poems written by Zen monks.

Most of the death poems by Zen monks that I have included in this collection are translated from *Zenso no Yuige* (Death poems of Zen priests) and *Zenso no Shoji* (Life and death of Zen priests) by Furuta Shokin (Tokyo: Shunjusha, 1965 and 1971). Ryokan's haiku also is from the former book.

Haiku death poems as such have not been gathered until now. Most of the poems whose sources are not stated in the Notes were taken from the biographical dictionary *Shinsen Haikai Nempyo* (Chronological chart of a new selection of *haikai*) edited by Hirabayashi Hoji and Onishi Kazuto (Osaka: Shoga Chimpon Zasshisha, 1923). Others were taken from older sources, indicated in the Notes; some of these are found only among the manuscripts of libraries and museums.

Few death poems have appeared in English translation. Several by Chinese and Japanese Zen monks are included in *Zen Poems of China and Japan* edited by Lucien Stryk and Takashi Ikemoto (New York: Anchor Books, 1973). Well-known tanka and haiku death-poems can occasionally be found in anthologies of Japanese poetry in translation.

❖ INDEX OF POETIC TERMS ❖

This index lists the words in the original Japanese haiku death-poems (Part III) discussed at least once in the commentaries, as well as many other words found in the poems. Reference is made to the poets' names. English translations of most of the words are cross-referenced to the Japanese words.

A few entries contain references to the poems of the Zen monks in Part II; the names of these poets are followed by "(Z)." Where two or more poets have names pronounced alike, references to them are followed by the date of death.

349

❖ GENERAL INDEX ❖

Because the death poems in this collection (Parts II and III) are presented by alphabetical order of the poets' names, these names are not included in this index, unless the poet is mentioned elsewhere in the text.